CARPETING SIMPLIFIED

Donald R. Brann

Library of Congress Card No. 72-91055

FOURTH PRINTING

Published by
EASI - BILD DIRECTIONS SIMPLIFIED, INC.
Briarcliff Manor, N.Y. 10510

FIRST PRINTING
© 1973

REVISED EDITIONS
1973, 1975, 1980

NOTE
Due to the variance in quality and availability of many materials and
products, always follow directions a manufacturer and/or retailer offers.
Unless products are used exactly as the manufacturer specifies, its war-
ranty can be voided. While the author mentions certain products by
trade name, no endorsement or end use guarantee is implied. In every
case the author suggests end uses as specified by the manufacturer prior
to publication.   The Publisher.

KNOWING HOW
MAKES DOING EASY

Learning to lay carpeting, like learning to live a fuller and more satisfying life, requires two basic ingredients currently in short supply — guts and a willingness to do something today you didn't think you could do yesterday. Installing carpet is something everyone can do, and do well, if they see well enough to read, possess an interest in living a fuller life, and are willing to make the physical effort.

Regardless of age, everyone must continue to learn. To stop means aging before your time. Millions now in their middle years currently face a period of deep depression because few learned how to live, or prepare for retirement. Having invested their adult years doggedly earning a living, they suddenly find themselves unwanted, and set adrift to "enjoy their golden years." Time hangs heavy. They find it difficult to make new and meaningful personal contacts. They feel neglected, outside looking in.

Consider installing carpet like making a deposit of effort in a bank called Experience. When you decide to retire, or someone decides for you, select one or a dozen different home improvement trades you have on deposit. See how easily, regardless of age, you can stay in the mainstream of society. Don't allow a streak of yellow or a mental block of laziness to prevent you from living a longer, happier life.

Don Brann

TABLE OF CONTENTS

READ, LEARN, TALK, THEN BUY

Installing carpet isn't a big deal. Like making love, it's something almost everyone can do, and do well, if they have the desire and the tools. To lay carpet like a pro requires professional tools and a willingness to check out all the preparatory steps. Unless the tools can be borrowed or rented, pay to have someone do the job. The tools needed are described in detail. Using each as directions suggest, doesn't require genius, or years of experience, it does require following simplified directions.

Doing anything you haven't done before, using muscles that haven't been used in years, can quicken a temper while it clouds your ability to think clearly. Since you are installing carpet to save your mind, or your money, there's no point in doing it, unless it can be done successfully. Learning any new skill is a beneficial experience for many different reasons. First, it requires overcoming fear; and secondly, it transforms you into a more creative and/or productive person. If you are a parent or teacher, it helps you help others while it opens doors to new job opportunities.

Since most physical effort helps release nervous tension, while it creates greater peace of mind, carpeting even a small room provides instant escape while it helps save a bundle improving your home. One word of caution: Don't start big. Regardless of where you need carpeting, start in a small room, even if none are on your carpeting schedule. Get acquainted with the tools, adhesives, seaming sealers, double faced tape, tackless strips or grippers, as they are called. Note the different way each kind of carpeting can be installed. Try out different installation methods. Apply cushion back carpeting with adhesive in a basement playroom; conventional back carpet and tackless grippers in a living room or hall, or with double faced tape; or adhesive, if you are installing carpeting in a kitchen or bathroom. Each method of installing carpet can be used in every kind of installation.

As you read through this book and get acquainted with the tools and materials the work requires, you'll develop an appreciation and understanding why each is needed. You will also appreciate how and why the many variables must be considered before purchasing carpet.

An under the carpet electrical surveillance mat, Illus. 208, is one of the best ways to protect an area adjacent to an entry door, sliding glass doors, a hallway, or any area that's vulnerable to a forced entry. See page 131.

The paper thin 30" wide mat is available in any length desired. It is cut to width of door opening plus 36" to 48". This protects 18" to 24" beyond edge of opening, Illus. 209, 211.

Tape mat to bare floor using double faced tape around its perimeter only. Connect wires from one mat to another, Illus. 210, then to protective circuit. The padding and carpeting is installed over the mat. Don't use staples to fasten carpeting in position.

Cover concrete floor with #15 felt before installing a mat.

When activated, the mat circuit triggers an alarm when anyone, even a cat or dog, walks over it. It will trigger whatever protective device, a bell, floodlights or telephone dialer that has been connected. The dialer can be programmed to alert the police, a security service, neighbor, etc.

Complete, easy to follow instructions for installing under the carpet surveillance mats are explained in Book #695.

While conventional carpet is normally installed with tackless strips, or double-faced tape, it can also be glued down. Cushion back sponge, foam, or indoor/outdoor, is installed with adhesive or tape. It is available in 54", 6', 9' and 12' widths. Your carpet retailer can help you zero in on the choice of carpet and method of installation. This decision will determine the tools and accessory items you will need.

Since each installation concerns a unique combination of problems, the author touches on certain steps briefly in the beginning, then explains the same step in detail in subsequent paragraphs. While a first reading will help you intelligently discuss many steps of installation with the retailer, knowing where to get specific instruction when you start the job, turns amateurs into pros.

Your carpet retailer can suggest the tools and adhesives needed, the amount of stretch the carpet you select requires, etc., etc. The tools shown are those most popular with the pros. Each was designed to simplify a particular step of installation in the easiest and quickest way.

For many practical reasons don't attempt even a small carpeting job until you have access to the tools. Then use each as the tool rental dealer or directions suggest.

The first important step to installing carpet requires an evaluation of the "ifs". This refers to the kind and condition of the floor, whether it's wood, linoleum, vinyl, asphalt, or ceramic tile; finished and waxed flooring, over wood joists or concrete; the kind of carpet to be installed and whether it is to be applied with adhesive, double faced tape, Illus. 1; or tackless strips, Illus. 2.

tape for → latex seams

←double faced tape

←pad tape

hot melt seaming tape →

←hot melt seaming tape

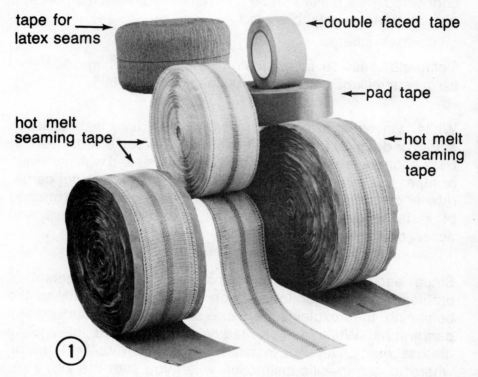

①

Other "ifs" concern walls being straight, corners square, floor level, etc., etc. You must make an examination of the floor, walls, doorways, etc., in the same interested and methodical manner an old fashioned doctor formerly examined a prompt paying patient. This inspection and analysis not only helps in selecting the proper carpeting, and padding where required, but also pays a bonus in years of carefree service.

When selecting a carpet with a pattern, consider direction of the pattern as it relates to normal traffic through a room. Also consider whether the pattern helps make the room seem larger or whether it crowds you in.

10

Installing carpet and doing it well pays many dividends. Besides saving a bundle, one of the richest rewards is the feeling of accomplishment. Since every house contains its own special combination of conditions, people and problems, it's important to read, then refer back to those steps that pertain to your job.

Because some words used to describe installation may sound a bit confusing, here are a few of the most commonly used.

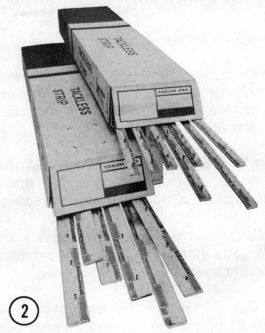

Installing carpet 1/4" or 1/2" HEAVY, refers to actual length or width needed, plus 1/4" or 1/2".

A CROSS JOINT describes adding to the length of carpet.

Each width of carpet is called a BREADTH. A breadth can be 54", 6', 9' or 12' depending on carpet purchased. When laying 54" carpet across a room twelve feet in width, sixteen feet in length, you would need four breadths.

The CARPET FIELD is the carpet you install, not the selvage edge you cut off.

A SEAM adds width to carpet.

STAIRS SOLID means both tread and riser is completely covered from one edge to the other.

UPHOLSTERY WORK refers to capping stairs, fitting through and around spindles, note: Illus. 138.

PILLOWING THE STAIRS refers to two layers of pad.

DRY FIT means no adhesive.

FILL-INS are recesses, doorways, toeboards, even closet floors that are to be carpeted. When installing carpet in a room where you want to include a closet floor, the fill-in could be included in overage, or by seam sealing.

Carpet has a SWEEP. The yarn lays down in one direction and stands up in the opposite direction. No matter how many breadths are installed, all must sweep in the same direction.

DOUBLE CUT refers to cutting two edges prior to making a seam. Both breadths are rolled out. One overlaps the other 2". Both breadths are then cut.

To TRACE CUT. Use a chalk line to snap a straight line approximately 2" from edge. Cut through back of conventional carpet. Position this breadth about 1½" from edge of second breadth and trace cut.

Using a razor blade knife, trace cut cushion back from face following a row of yarn that provides a matching seam.

SEAM SEALING

Seam sealing means exactly what the two words indicate, but there are several ways this can be accomplished. It can be done with adhesive as described on page 42; with tape as mentioned on page105;or sewn, page107.Seam sealing requires no great skill. It does require following directions, and using proper adhesive. And don't try using the wrong adhesive because you happen to have some left over. The adhesives manufactured for installing carpet greatly simplify the work each was designed for. But—DON'T EXPERIMENT.

Read this book through at least once, twice if necessary before selecting carpet. Discuss method of installation with the retailer. Explain where it's to be installed, kind and condition of floor, etc. How a retailer reacts to your questions is important. Since you will be able to ask intelligent questions, there's no reason why the retailer can't explain any step that needs clarifying. It's at this point an experienced and cooperative retailer can save you a lot of money even when you pay top dollar for the carpet.

When you explain where the carpet is to be installed, and question the need for padding, underlayment, and/or the advisability of running the same carpet in two or more rooms, a smart retailer will attempt to cinch the sale by making a date to inspect the area, even when you plan on installing the carpet. He can, in minutes, tell you much that can prevent your making mistakes. But to understand what he is talking about, to intelligently follow his advice—"READ".

When he inspects the area to be carpeted, he can double check your estimate, suggest exact amount of carpet, adhesive, seam sealer, tackless grippers, also explain any special problem, i.e., an alcove, stairs, etc.

Buying carpet is frequently a once or twice in a lifetime purchase. For this reason, get mileage out of the purchase. And the time to get it, is before you buy. Shop, talk, then decide which retailer is most interested in zeroing in on your problem. Don't allow the price of the carpet to dictate where you buy. Your primary concern is to purchase a quality carpet and to make an equal quality installation.

Carpeting is an extremely good long term investment. Since it's inevitable that one or more places may wear faster than others, buy some extra yardage. Keep it wrapped and mothproofed. When needed it will be almost priceless.

Since considerable money can be saved by installing it yourself, the retailer who measures the area, and takes time to answer any installation problem, earns your business. For these reasons always shop for carpet when the retailer has time to talk, and when it comes to buying carpet, learn to listen well.

Another important element that should be given prime consideration concerns your physical and mental capability to do the job. Unless you feel physically fit to jockey a bulky item around, and subconsciously feel you can keep your cool if you get tired half way through, don't attempt it. Always stop when you get tired. Don't start if you need to hurry, or meet a deadline.

If you are installing cushion back, or indoor/outdoor carpet in a room where a starting wall is straight, a corner 90°, the shoe molding, Illus.3, furniture, and everything else removed, the floor smooth, level, structurally sound; dust, dirt, paint and wax free; it's fairly easy to measure the area, and purchase sufficient carpet to cut each breadth 3" longer than width of room, then install it with the kind of adhesive dealer recommends. Sand off all paint on a floor before applying adhesive. A gallon of adhesive will frequently do a room approximately 12' x 12'. Since you seldom find a straight wall, or a 90° corner, it's best to proceed as directions suggest.

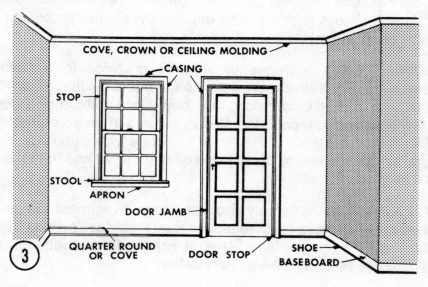

14

Carpet can be installed in many different ways, over many different kinds of floor surfaces. The first step is to zero in on the kind of carpet you feel compliments the room. While conventional back carpet can be installed with or without a pad, no padding is used with cushion back, sponge, foam or indoor/outdoor.

Choosing the right carpet for a specific area is an important first step. A good carpet is a long term investment in comfort, soundproofing, convenience and decor. Choose wool, nylon, polyester or acrylic. All compliment the decor and increase the value of your home.

SURFACE INSPECTION

Carpeting can be installed over concrete, ceramic, vinyl asbestos or asphalt tile, over new and old wood floors, indoors as well as outdoors, over metal or wood decks. Your carpet retailer will recommend type of carpet and adhesive best suited for the surface you describe, but he can't answer too many questions unless he inspects the area to be covered.

To advise intelligently, he would have to know what you must find out, i.e., condition of surface. If it's over a hardwood floor covered with a build-up of wax, and/or badly warped because of dampness; over worn linoleum that's badly damaged and needs removal; directly over vinyl or asphalt tile, where dampness has loosened or curled some of the tiles; or whether you plan on carpeting over subflooring that might have a seasonal tendency to expand, or contract, or absorb ground moisture.

To ascertain the exact shape of the area to be carpeted, to determine whether walls are straight and corners are square, measure across room at both ends, and again at center. If a doorway, closet floor, or any adjoining area requires an extra long breadth, make note where, when and length needed. Don't take one width measurement and assume the entire room measures the same. To ascertain whether floor is level, select a

15

straight 2 x 6 x 8' or 2 x 6 x 10'. To select a straight one, sight down one edge to see if it bows in or out, or crowns up. Place a level on the 2 x 6, Illus. 4, and move it over the floor.

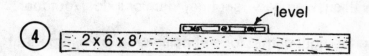

If level indicates a slope, raise one end and check amount of space between the floor and the bottom edge of 2 x 6. This will tell you where and how much build up the floor needs to be leveled. In many cases, no underlayment other than latex floor patching may be required. A shallow slope can frequently be corrected with one or two layers of latex patch. This can be spread feather thin to ¼" thick in one coat, Illus. 5. Any number of coats can be applied to build up to height required. Follow manufacturer's directions and allow each layer to set time prescribed.

Latex underlayment can be used to level floor covered by panelboard; and /or where tackless is used. Some carpet adhesives don't bond to latex underlayment, use with discretion.

16

A concrete basement floor presently covered with tight, smooth vinyl or asphalt tile, one that doesn't show any water stains, or condensation marks, can be covered with carpeting using adhesive, after all existing wax build up has been removed. Wash floor with a commercial solvent.

If floor tile is cracked, curled, or beginning to loosen, remove all loose tile and smooth surface with latex underlayment or flakeboard manufactured with waterproof glue; or exterior grade plywood, or other moisture resistant panelboard specified for basement floor installation. Always use an underlayment that's guaranteed for the area in which you plan on using it. If only a few tiles are missing, or badly curled, you can sand off high spots and fill in low ones with latex underlayment.

While many developers of low and medium priced houses use plyscord as underlayment on upper floors, and find it satisfactory, it isn't recommended below grade where it's subject to dampness. Only exterior grade plywood or moisture resistant underlayment should be used. If in doubt, play safe. Before laying underlayment in a damp area, cover entire floor with #15 felt embedded in asphalt cement, Illus. 6. Allow felt to come up walls 3" or 4". This can be cut off after underlayment has been installed.

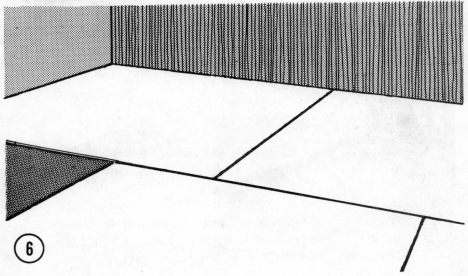

6

Underlayment is available in 4' x 4' or 4' x 8' panels, ½", ⅝" or ¾" thick. Use underlayment wherever a smooth surface is required. Many pros embed the underlayment panels in asphalt cement directly over concrete. No felt is used. The asphalt cement is used as a sealant.

When installing underlayment over a wood floor, nail underlayment every 6" along edges, every 12" along floor joists. Underlayment can be nailed to a concrete floor using special nails, but this tends to compound the negative. The more nails you drive into a concrete slab the more chances you have for cracks and holes.

CAUTION: Since builders frequently embed copper water or hot water heating lines in a concrete slab, never drill holes or drive nails until you ascertain location of a line.

When panelboard underlayment needs to be applied, it's first necessary to remove doors. Doors must be refitted by sawing off across bottom edge. Sandpaper to smooth edge.

The first step in preparing any room for a wall-to-wall carpeting job is to remove everything from the room that isn't nailed down. Then remove the shoe molding or quarter round, Illus. 3, from the entire room. Use a 1" chisel to raise molding at center of room, then work your way toward the mitered corners. Remove all nails. If room contains a coved baseboard, Illus. 7, use the razor blade knife, Illus. 8, and cut off cove.

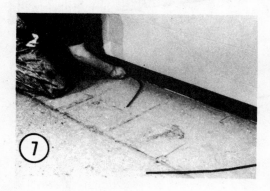

As you crawl around the floor, it's important to note any damaged, loose, or squeaky flooring that needs repair before proceeding. Unless wood flooring is nailed securely, and provides a solid, squeak-free floor, the carpet will have little chance of survival.

If you are modernizing an old house where the floor has had it, consider covering with ⅜" plyscord, or exterior grade plywood (in basements), or ½" or ⅝" underlayment. Use thickness required to level and stiffen floor and to overcome all spring or movement.

If existing flooring only needs a few nails here and there to tighten up loose boards, use 8 penny finishing nails. Drive these through flooring into floor joists. Countersink heads.

If flooring appears to be tightly nailed, but the floor still has a noticeable sag or spring, your problem may be in one or more weakened floor joists. Inspect joists, Illus. 9.

SOLID BRIDGING

CROSS BRIDGING

9

To raise a sagging joist, use a jack and 4 x 4, or a screw jack lally column, Illus. 10. Using a level on a 2 x 6, Illus. 4, watch the level when the jack raises joist. Determine whether you can stiffen joist by nailing a matching length of the same size lumber to one or both sides of original joist, Illus. 11; or whether a lally column is all that's needed.

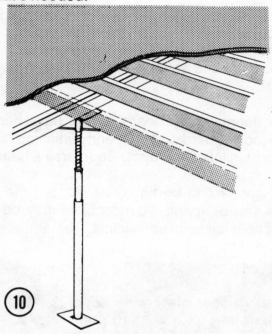

If floor is solid, but has a noticeable low area, you can spread latex underlayment to raise and level. This preparation is vitally important to installing carpet successfully. Even if you chicken out and don't lay the carpet, you can still save a bundle stiffening and leveling up the floor.

If hardwood flooring has a tendency to sag or spring, and there are no loose or damaged boards, go into the basement. Ask someone to walk on the questionable area while you evaluate what's happening below. You might find it necessary to drive a wedge between floor joist and loose flooring, or between joist and foundation. Or you may find one or more rotted or weakened floor joists that need replacement or reinforcement with gusset plates, Illus. 11.

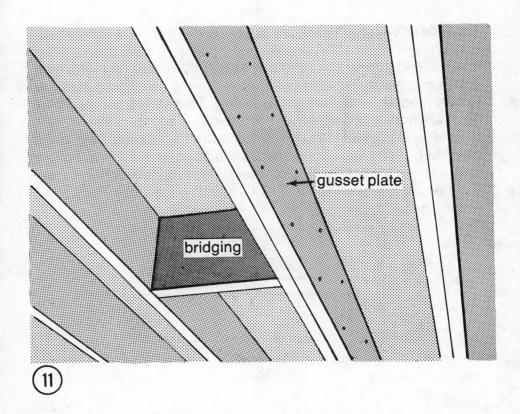

gusset plate

bridging

11

Use length gusset plate needed to remove all movement. Spike to existing joist with 16 penny nails.

After washing or sanding off a wax buildup, carpet can be applied over a wood floor with adhesive, or doublefaced tape, or with tackless strips. The choice of adhesive depends on the surface covered and material installed. Always use adhesive recommended both for the surface you are covering and the carpet you have selected.

Carpet cement is formulated for various end uses. Latex adhesive is recommended for installing sponge-backed, foam-backed, as well as indoor/outdoor, jute backed and manmade backing. It spreads easily, has a long open time which eliminates rush, and is water resistant-freeze-thaw stable. One brand, rated non-freeze sensitive, is ideally suited for basement installations below grade. Note page 136.

PADDING—UNDERLAYMENTS

If you are installing conventional back carpet over padding, over concrete, your retailer will recommend a flammable or nonflammable pad cement specially formulated for padding. This anchors padding to all hard surface floors, prevents pad from slipping when carpet is stretched. This cement will bond hair, rubberized felt, sponge rubber padding, or combination hair and jute padding to concrete, metal decking, marble, terrazzo, vinyl or asphalt tile. Apply with a straight edged trowel, Illus. 12 no notches. Note page 133.

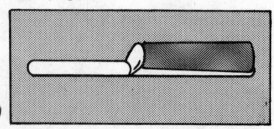

When installing bubble rubber padding, the scrim or felt back is up, bubbles down, Illus. 13. The bubbles trap air, give padding resiliency.

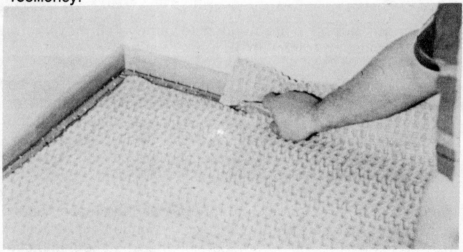

Always cut padding net to tackless. When applying carpet with tape, cut padding net to tape.

SEAMING PAD

Use 2" pad tape to tape seams, Illus. 14. This lessens chance for dust to streak through seam into carpet. Apply tape to top of seam, then reinforce taped seam with a few strips crosswise, Illus. 15. Drive 9/16 staples every 6" along both outside edges of the tape, full length of seam, also through cross strips to hold padding in position to a wood floor.

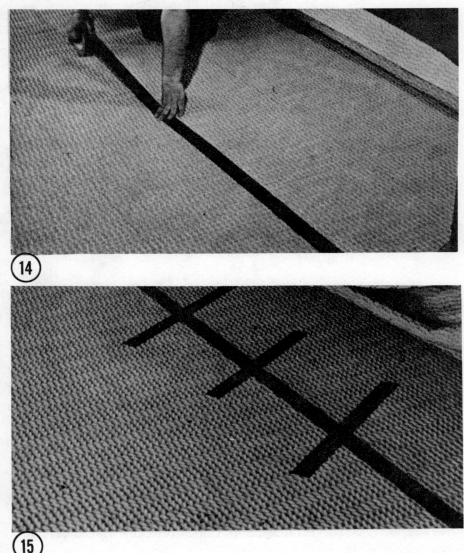

14

15

Always remove pins from door hinges, Illus. 16. Remove saddle Illus. 3, if you plan on running padding and/or carpeting into a closet or adjoining room.

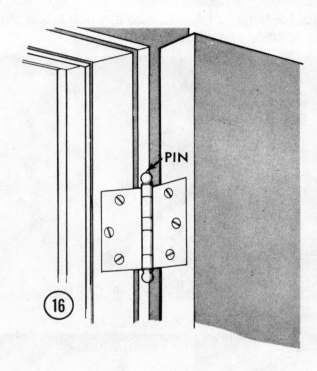

PIN

16

While four walls make a room, few walls are straight, few corners square. Since the wall trimmer cuts the carpet following shape of wall, your only problem is to allow 1½ to 2" of carpet to lap each wall.

The alert carpet retailer will either rent all the tools needed for the carpet you select, or will recommend a tool rental store. It's essential you obtain all the tools, and equally important you know how to use each. Don't practice using an unfamiliar tool on the carpet you plan on installing. Either practice on old carpet or buy sample rejects.

24

If you plan on doing a small job and want to keep your initial investment down to a minimum, buy a beginner's carpet installation kit, Illus. 17. This sells for around $10.00 and can pay for itself on the first job. The razor blade knife has a handle designed for cutting carpet. The kit contains a package of blades, seam sealer, seam solvent, a chalk line and chalk, double-faced vinyl tape, plus instructions that explain how to use each item.

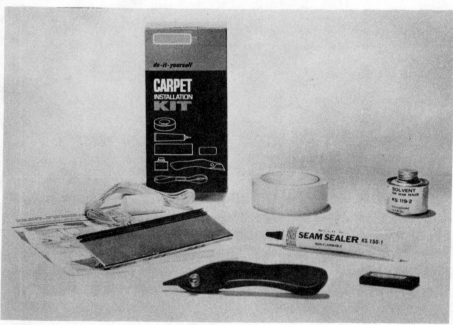

(17)

TOOLS REQUIRED FOR INSTALLING CUSHION BACK, INDOOR/OUTDOOR

To install woven cushion back carpet, or indoor/outdoor, you will need a Cushion Back Seam Cutter, Illus. 18. This cutter simplifies cutting all types of cushion backed carpet. The bottom is tapered to a Vee so it can follow between a row of yarn. The four sided blade makes clean cuts through hi-density foam or sponge backing. When you retract the blade, the Vee shaped bottom can be used to separate and open up a row of yarn. This permits cutting without splitting loops, Illus. 18. Woven cushion back carpet construction has a selvage edge made up of two rows of different colored face yarn.

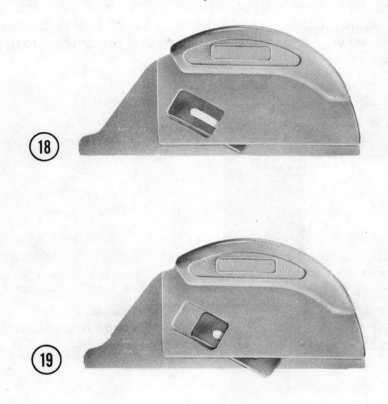

(18)

(19)

When you set the blade to depth needed to cut, it cuts close on blade side, Illus. 19, 20.

(20)

Another tool needed for this application is the **Razor Blade Knife**, Illus. 8. The handle of this knife places the blade at exact angle required for cutting high density foam carpet. Use this knife when back cutting conventional backed carpet, or face cutting cushion back.

To spread adhesive use a 3/32" notched trowel, Illus. 21.

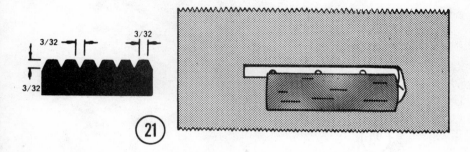

To trim rubber back, sponge, foam and vinyl-backed, also indoor/outdoor against the wall, use the **Wall Trimmer**, Illus. 22. The handle on this trimmer locks into three different positions. After setting blade to depth of cut, you can cut in either direction. Always set the blade on the Wall Trimmer approximately 1/16" less than thickness of carpet, unless trimmer manufacturer specifies otherwise.

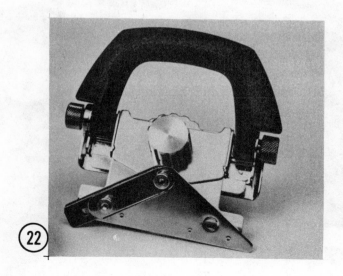

27

The Scribe Cutter, Illus. 23, provides a simple fool-proof way to face cut conventional back carpet so seams match perfectly. With this cutter, one piece of carpet can be cemented in postion, the other loose; or both pieces can be loose. You can also use this tool to cut any shape required.

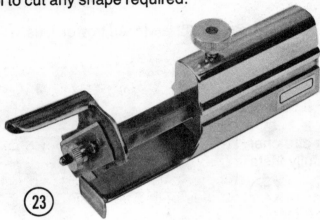

You will also need a miter box and hacksaw if you need to install any metal mouldings, a stapler, chalk line, carpet shears, screwdriver and hammer, Illus. 24.

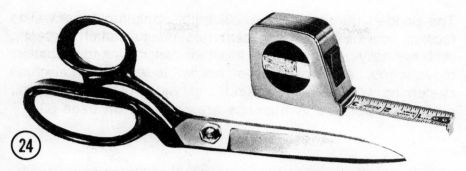

(24)

TOOLS REQUIRED FOR CONVENTIONAL BACK CARPET INSTALLATION

The carpet stretcher, and a kicker, Illus. 25, 27, provide the key to successfully installing conventional back carpet. The stretcher shown has a 14" wide head containing up to 60 teeth. The extra sets of extension tubes permit using stretcher in an area from 33" to 22 feet.

The padded tail block, Illus. 26, butts up against walls. The handle provides all the stretch needed to install carpeting professionally. How you use this tool can insure the success of your job. Ask your carpet retailer to explain how much stretch he advises for the kind and width of carpeting you purchase. Detailed instructions are provided on page 62.

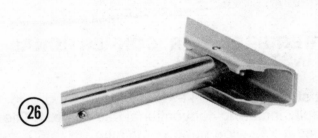

The Kicker, Illus. 27, fastens carpet to tackless in those areas suggested.

You will need a Wall Trimmer, Illus. 28. This has a one knob control for in and out - up and down adjustments, cuts both ways, angled arm reduces marking wall. The guide toe pushes edge of carpet into gully.

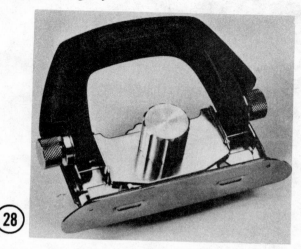

Other tools needed are an awl, Illus. 29; chalk line, Illus. 30; flexible straight edge, Illus. 31; rubber mallet, Illus. 32; stapler, Illus. 33, stair tool, Illus. 34; razor blade knife, Illus. 8; strip cutter, Illus. 35; miter box and hammer, and a spreader, Illus. 36.

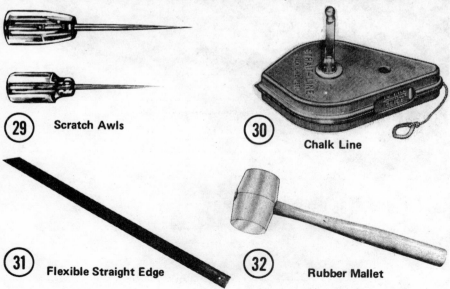

Scratch Awls

Chalk Line

Flexible Straight Edge

Rubber Mallet

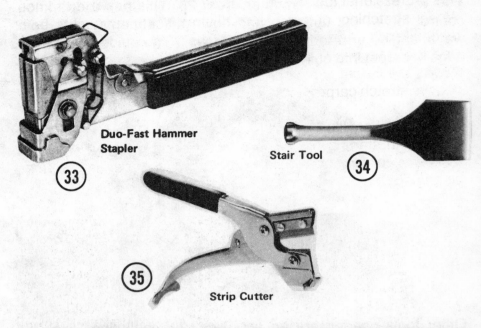

Duo-Fast Hammer Stapler

(33)

Stair Tool

(34)

(35)

Strip Cutter

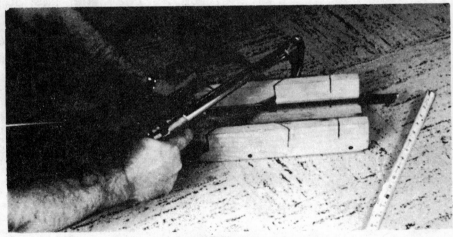

(36)

Spreader

32

The professional tools used to install carpeting are easy to use. When stretching carpet, always stretch the amount retailer recommends. Always release handle of the stretcher slowly. Use the spreader to push carpet into gully and onto pins, Illus. 92. As the carpet moves back it hooks carpet firmly to tackless. Always stretch carpet following procedure shown, Illus. 93.

Use the kicker, Illus. 37, to kick conventional back carpet onto tackless in starting corner. Rub carpet onto pins with hammer. Installing conventional back carpeting to tackless is explained on page 58.

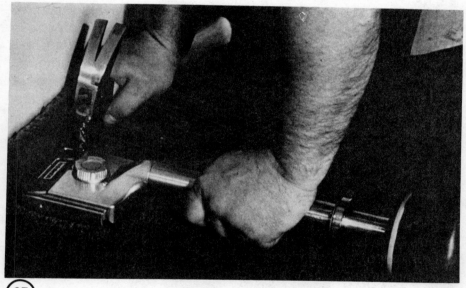

(37)

INSTALLATION USING DOUBLE FACED TAPE CUSHION BACK OR INDOOR/OUTDOOR CARPET

Double faced tape, designed especially for installing carpet, Illus. 1, is available 1½" in width, in 14 ft. rolls, also in 2" width x 36 yd. rolls. Carpet can be taped to any structurally sound floor that's wax, dirt, dust or paint free. Remove furniture, base moulding, etc. Sand wax or paint off area where tape is to be applied.

(38)

Prior to purchase, inquire whether the carpet measures a full 54", 6' or 12'. Ask the retailer to roll out and measure width at a number of places along a long length. After delivery again roll out the carpet and check width carefully, Illus. 38. Carpet can vary as much as one inch in width. When laying 54" carpet, it doesn't take many breadths to change the needed amount. If the carpet has been stored standing up, the selvage edge may be compressed and so uneven it could require a wide first cut, Illus. 39.

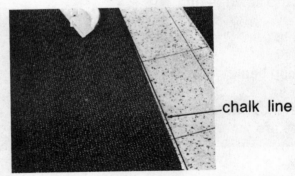

chalk line

(39)

After preparing floor area as previously described, roll out the carpet and carefully measure width at a number of different places. This will give you some idea how much you may have to cut to achieve a straight edge.

While a selvage edge can be lapped 1½" on the starting wall, then trimmed to fit wall; when making a seam, you have to cut off the selvage edge, Illus. 40. If you have a straight wall, you can unroll 54" carpet, snap a chalk line at 52", cut carpet and butt it against the wall.

34

(40)

CAUTION: When you lay out the carpet and find an uneven selvage edge due to its being improperly handled, call your carpet retailer. It's at this time you can voice a legitimate complaint unless you purchased carpet "at a price" from a fast buck retailer.

Snap a chalk line on the floor, Illus. 39. Lay the first breadth along this line. This will show you how the selvage edge lays. Or you can unroll a long length and snap a chalk line 1" or 1½" in from the selvage edge. Measure in from edge at various points. If it bows in at any point, it will be necessary to snap a chalk line sufficient distance from deepest point to cut a straight edge. Use the seam cutter, Illus. 18, to open up a row of yarn before cutting cushion back.

Always cut at least one row of field yarn off with the selvage. There are times when you need to cut one row on one side, and two rows of field yarn off other selvage edge in order to match the color on the adjoining breadth. Unless you do this, you could create a light or dark streak. If you are laying a pattern, it's essential you plan your cut so the pattern matches perfectly.

The same procedure is used when a selvage edge isn't present. Always double check to be sure that two rows of the same color yarn will not be joined together. After cutting one breadth of carpeting, unroll the next one and check for shading, Illus. 41. If the breadth looks dark, switch it. The blue line on the back is a directional mark that tells which way the carpet is running. If two lines are together, one breadth needs to be reversed.

35

The blade on the seam cutter is first retracted and the Vee shaped bottom is used to separate the yarn and open a row to permit cutting.

The tool is marked "cuts close this side". This positions blade against edge that becomes a seam. Set blade so it cuts 1/16 less than thickness required. Cut each breadth to be seamed together in opposite directions.

Cut each breadth 3" longer than width of room. This allows 1½" at each end. Unroll next breadth but before cutting, check for shading.

Strip covering off one face of tape and press tape close to wall around entire perimeter of room, Illus. 42. At doorways use two lengths, one alongside the other, to provide a 3" or 4" band of tape. Run a strip down center of room.

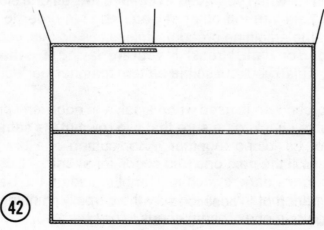

Do not remove paper covering on topside of tape. Position carpet allowing 1½", or amount of overage needed to take care of any irregularities in walls, or fillins. When carpet has been positioned accurately, place several heavy objects on top to hold it in position; or use great care not to move it out of position.

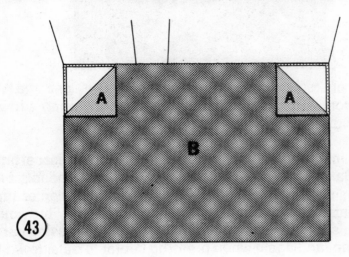

Carefully fold back corners A, Illus. 43. Then carefully fold back B, Illus. 44.

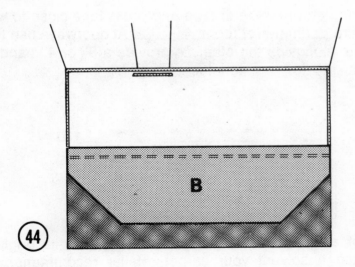

Strip paper off top of exposed tape, and carefully position carpet on tape. Start at center and work towards end.

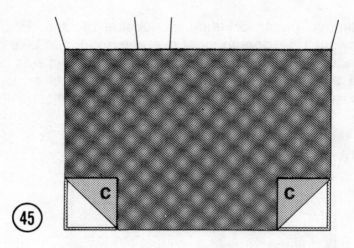

45

Remember, carpet must lap wall about 1½". Press carpet firmly into tape. Carefully fold back corners C, Illus. 45, and fold back D, Illus. 46, and again E, Illus. 47. This exposes center tape. Remove paper from top and repeat procedure previously outlined. Be sure to eliminate all wrinkles before pressing carpet to center tape, and again when pressing center to outside wall.

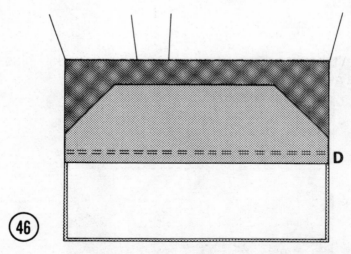

46

If you goof and discover the carpet moved from its original position, use a solvent your carpet retailer recommends to remove tape from floor. Don't attempt to lift carpet by pulling it away from tape.

38

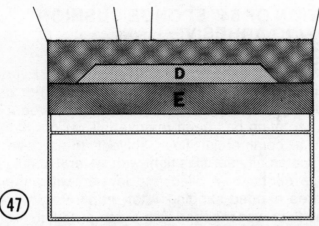

47

Using a screwdriver or stair tool, crease carpet to wall, Illus. 48. Using the wall trimmer recommended for carpet being installed, trim carpet net.

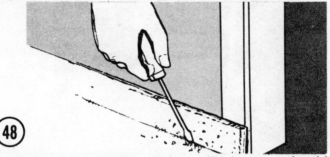

48

If you don't have access to a wall trimmer, the kit, Illus. 17, contains a guide plate and razor knife,

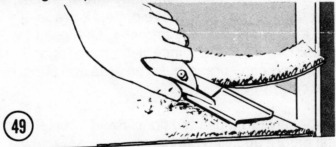

49

To trim carpet at the wall, use the guide plate. After creasing carpet with a screwdriver, place the plate with the highest leg tight against the excess carpet on wall, Illus. 49. With blade of knife riding on leg, cut excess. If too much is left after this cut, reverse the trimmer plate. Use the short leg and cut again.

INSTALLATION OF 54" SPONGE CUSHION CARPET USING ADHESIVE

Illus. 50, shows a vinyl asbestos floor over concrete. Everything in the room has been removed. The shoe molding or quarter round, the door and saddle between the two areas being covered with carpeting has been removed. The floor has been cleaned with a commercial floor solvent to remove wax. Inspection indicates all floor tiles tight with several small pieces missing. These spots were filled and leveled with latex floor patch.* One area needed sanding. After preparatory work was completed, the floor was mopped with a damp cloth to eliminate dust and dirt.

You will normally need two adhesives when installing sponge cushion carpeting. One is a non-flammable, freeze-thaw, stable latex adhesive that can be used above or below grade. It's water resistant once it's permitted to dry properly. One gallon will do a room approximately 12 x 12. Since it has an "open" time of about one hour, you can spread quite an area and still take your time laying the carpet.

Never apply adhesive to a painted floor. Sand floor. Remove all paint and dust before applying adhesive.

Also needed is a Seam Sealer, and a can of Solvent to remove any excess seam solvent. Never apply solvent directly to face of cushion back. The solvent will destroy the foam or sponge. Use a white cloth to clean seam sealer from face of carpet.

* Use patching compatible to adhesive dealer recommends.

TRIM AND DRY FIT CARPET

The seam cutter, Illus 18, cuts close on one side. Cut edge of each breadth in opposite directions. If the selvage edge isn't cut through completely, turn the selvage under and pull off waste, Illus. 51.

To seam carpet it's first necessary to check the sweep on both breadths to make certain the carpet is laying properly. The seam edge that sweeps away from the seam is set into the adhesive first so no face yarn overlaps seam.

Follow the same layout and cutting procedure when there's no selvage edge.

After the seam edge of the first breadth has been trimmed and the breadth positioned on floor so it provides sufficient overage to be fitted to wall, draw a line on floor to indicate position of seam, Illus. 52.

After trimming selvage edge of second breadth, and after carefully noting whether rows at seam match, overlap second breadth ¼" to permit making a compression seam, Illus. 53.

With both breadths in exact position determined when dry fitted, fold each back, Illus. 54. Use care not to move either breadth out of position.

Using a 3/32" notched trowel, Illus. 21, spread adhesive over drawn line first, Illus. 55. Work from center out towards walls.

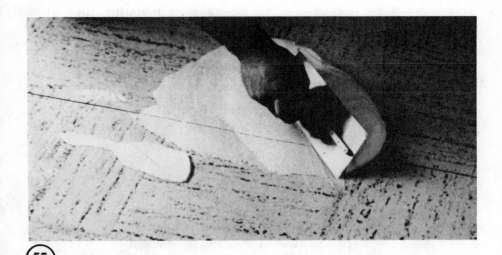

Spread adhesive evenly over exposed floor area, Illus. 56. Leave no globs or ridges and make certain pencil line remains visible. Try to end adhesive in a reasonably straight line along folds. Always use trowel notched to size adhesive manufacturer specifies. The tooth depth can be increased with a three cornered file. The depth can be decreased by wrapping tape across both faces of teeth.

(56)

The first section (not the overlapping breadth) is set into adhesive, center first, Illus. 57, then worked out towards ends. This method eliminates air pockets.

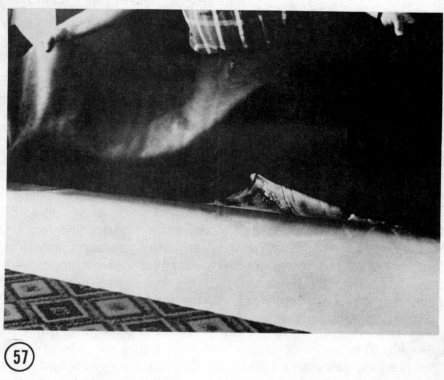

(57)

Use the cardboard core from the carpet to roll out ripples, Illus. 58.

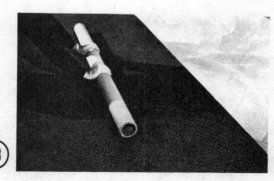

(58)

The next and very important step is to apply the Seam Sealer to the seam edge of the first breadth of carpet, Illus. 59.

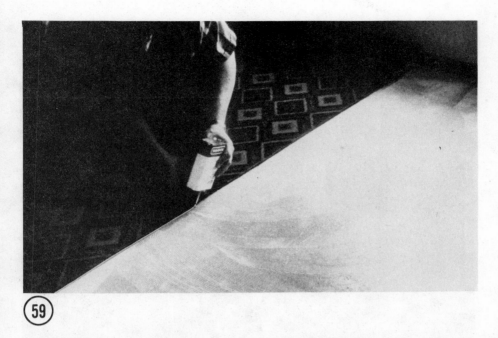

(59)

The Seam Sealer is applied from side of nozzle, Illus. 60, and not the tip, Illus. 61. The tip of the nozzle glides on floor while notch in side of nozzle feeds a bead onto the base of the primary back. Unless you cut the nozzle at proper height, and make the opening to size needed, you could run into a lot of trouble. For this reason, ask your carpet retailer to show you how and where to cut the nozzle, and/or supply an extra nozzle for practice. Also read directions on Seam Sealer you purchase.

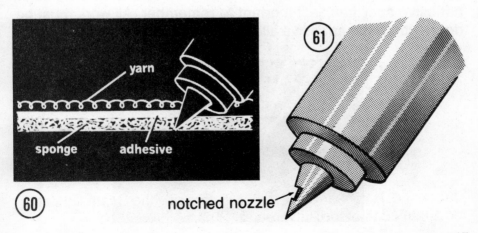

yarn

sponge   adhesive

(60)

(61)

notched nozzle

After the seam sealer has been applied, the second section, the one with the ¼" overlap, is positioned center first, Illus. 62.

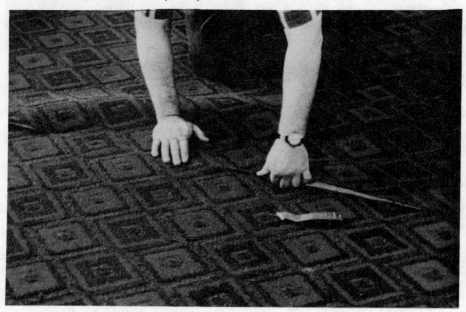

62

The pucker noted in Illus. 63, is created from the overlap. The compression this exerts helps hold the seam together until sealer sets. Rub the excess carpet across the floor away from the seam. As mentioned on page 40, the open time floor adhesive specifies, is important to remember. All work must be done within time adhesive allows.

63

Rub all ripples out toward the wall. Next, crease the carpet at wall using a stair tool or screw driver, Illus. 34, 64. Creasing the carpet is important. The wall trimmer, Illus. 22, 65, not only cuts the carpet net to the wall or baseboard, but also follows any irregularities in the wall. The three position handle permits cutting in both directions without changing position of blade.

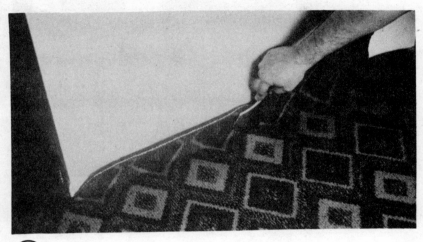

After the excess carpet has been cut, push an awl, Illus. 29, 66, down between edge of wall or baseboard and pull it through the cut. This rolls loops of yarn under and leaves a smooth finished edge at baseboard.

66

If you work through two or more days and face a situation where one breadth has been cemented completely to edge, Illus. 67, the compression method can still be followed but it's wise to use a clean trowel to keep face of yarn free of adhesive. Remember, it's only necessary to apply Seam Sealer to one edge.

67

Should a seam open, use a piece of Velcro tape or stay tack, Illus. 68, to hold seam together until adhesive has a chance to set.

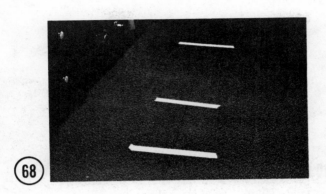

Cutting and fitting carpet under a toe space is accomplished in the same way it's done along a wall. Always crease the carpet before trimming. Set the blade on the wall trimmer approximately 1/16" less than the thickness of carpet. Always push forward and towards the wall.

If you have to make a cross joint, Illus. 69, make a straight cut on one breadth using the Seam Cutter. Overlap carpet at least 2", or amount pattern requires, and trace cut the overlapping breadth. These cuts are always made dry, no adhesive.

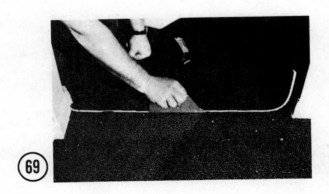

Always crease carpet at wall, Illus. 70, before using the wall trimmer, Illus. 71. Place an awl in position shown, Illus. 72, and pull it through. This turns ends of yarn under.

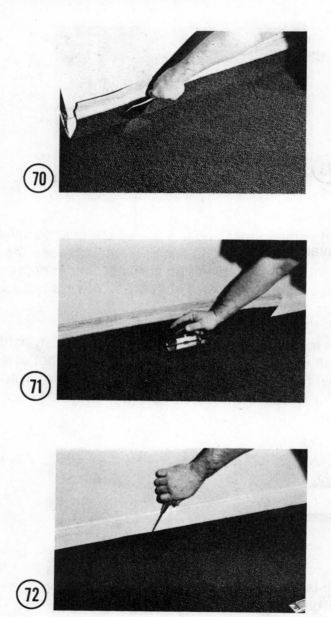

Always rough cut carpet around a post, Illus. 73, so it lays flat. Do this dry, no adhesive. Use the trimmer, Illus. 22, to cut carpet net around post after setting in adhesive.

At doorways, or where carpet ends, and other types of flooring begin, use one of the many specially designed mouldings, Illus. 74, available from your carpet retailer.

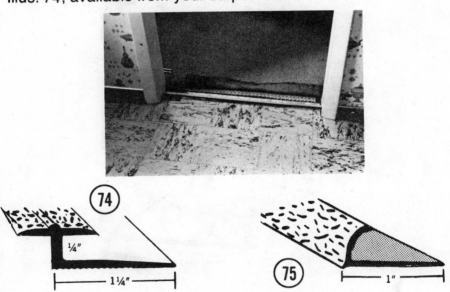

Illus. 75, shows one type of moulding recommended for cushion back. This is always nailed to floor prior to spreading adhesive. The wide base is covered with adhesive. The adhesive holds carpet to moulding. The lip is hammered down with a rubber mallet, Illus. 32. Note mouldings on pages 137, 138.

Always cut carpet heavy when installing a moulding. Using the razor blade knife, Illus. 8, cut carpet two or three rows of yarn heavy. This allows carpet to fit under lip. Rub the excess carpet under the lip using the stair tool, Illus. 34. The tap down lip doesn't hold the carpet. The adhesive does this. The lip protects the edge.

Since conventional back carpet is stretched, while cushion back is glued , there is no practical way to seam the two, Illus. 76. In this case a T-shaped moulding, Illus. 77, can be installed. This has pins on one side to receive conventional back, while the cushion back is fastened to floor with adhesive. Both lips are then hammered down. This is nailed to floor before installing cushion back.

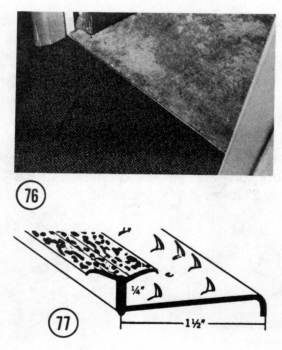

A binder bar, Illus. 78, is used in a sliding door installation, Illus. 79. This is installed after cushion back has been cemented to floor.

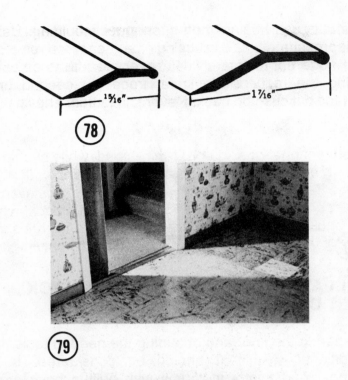

78

79

SEAMING - INDOOR/OUTDOOR

To accurately match two breadths, you can either double cut indoor/outdoor, or trace cut. To double cut, overlap one edge approximately 2" and cut both breadths, Illus. 80, in one cut.

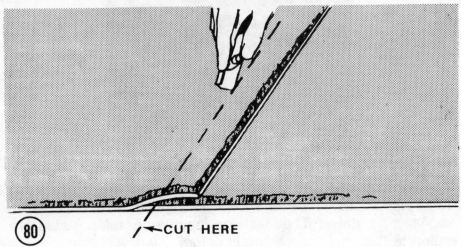

80 → CUT HERE

To trace cut cushion back tufted, snap a chalk line and cut one edge approximately 2" in using the seam cutter. Position trimmed edge approximately 1½" over breadth to be cut, Illus. 81. Using the razor blade knife, trace cut second breadth. Always face cut cushion back. Never join factory edges.

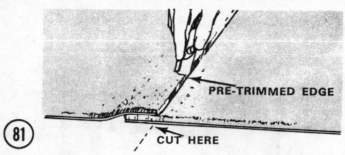

PRE-TRIMMED EDGE

(81) CUT HERE

INSTALLATION OF CONVENTIONAL BACK CARPET USING TACKLESS STRIPS.

After preparing the floor and obtaining the needed tools there is one additional step that should be considered. In many installations, particularly in rooms with built-in base cabinets, you may want carpet to cover toeboard, Illus. 82. When you lay carpet rough, add amount needed to cover toe board.

(82)

Tackless strips come in four foot lengths and are predrilled. Manufacturer supplies nails. If you plan on installing tackless strips with adhesive, be sure to remove wax from surface before applying adhesive. The four foot lengths of tackless strip are nailed to floor around perimeter of room, Illus. 83.

54

(83)

Illus. 84, shows a typical installation. Wall A was the straightest; corner AB almost square. The shoe molding was removed. Inspection indicated a satisfactory surface that required no leveling or structural repair. While tackless strip can be nailed to wood or concrete floors, adhesive can also be used to attach tackless strips to concrete, steel, marble, wood or terrazzo. Always cut tackless to 6" strips when installing with adhesive.

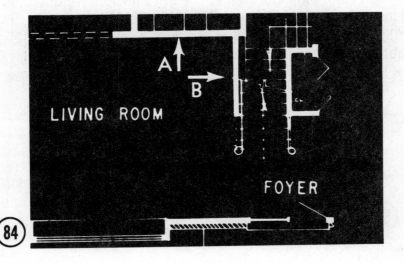

(84)

It's important to use adhesive the retailer recommends for each step, and to use it exactly as the manufacturer specifies.

Most pros start with one straight wall and one square corner, Illus. 85. When laying conventional back carpet with tackless strips, they position tackless away from wall, according to the thickness of carpet being installed.

85

Tackless strip, Illus. 2 ranges from 1" to 1⅞" wide, 4 ft. in length, and are available in three different pin heights ranging from ¼", 3/16" to 7/32", Illus. 86. Use ¼" height with light weight padding and low pile carpet with heavy backing. Use the 3/16" pin height with light weight padding and medium backing. Use 7/32" pin height with light weight padding and scrim backed or high pile carpeting.

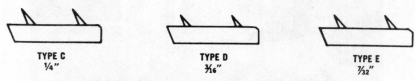

TYPE C	TYPE D	TYPE E
¼"	³⁄₁₆"	⁷⁄₃₂"

TYPE C-1/4" pin — use with high pile carpets with double backing.

TYPE D-3/16" pin — use with low profile carpets and/or single back construction.

86

TYPE E-7/32" pin — use with double backing and medium or high pile carpets.

TACKLESS Strips come in nine different types. Standard tackless strip is 9/32" thick and is recommended for installation over wood, concrete, tile, terrazzo, marble, etc. It can be nailed or cemented with tackless strip cement. 3/8" thick tackless is also available where 100 ozs. padding is being installed.

Pre-nailed tackless strip, 9/32" thick, in 4 ft. length is sold with twelve preset Ring Shank nails. These are equally spaced to assure a firm installation.

Your carpet retailer can recommend the tackless strip pin height best suited for the carpet and padding you select.

Use a cutter, Illus. 35, 87, to cut tackless. Always let the cutter do the work. On most cutters, the bottom leg rests on the floor. The strip is cut by pushing the top handle down, rather than by squeezing as one does when using metal snips.

(87)

NOTE: If you are installing tackless in a room containing a cove edged rubber, vinyl or linoleum base, cut the cove, Illus. 7. Use the razor blade knife.

APPLYING TACKLESS TO CONCRETE

Fasten tackless with nails supplied. Even when these hold, the strip should be reinforced by drilling and nailing every foot. If the pre-nails aren't holding, drill the tackless every 6". Use a 3/16" carbide tip bit or ⅛" solid carbide bit with a rotary type of hammer drill, Illus. 88, cut tackless to 6" lengths when applying to rough concrete.

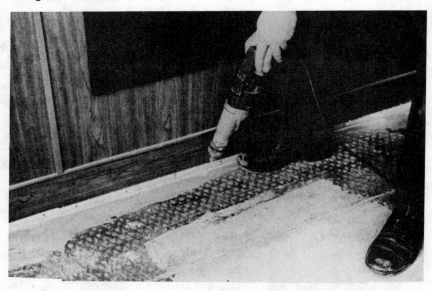

Always drill holes in concrete slightly deeper than length of nail. This permits driving nails deep enough so head of nail finishes flush. Always use a nail that's slightly oversized (in diameter) from the hole drilled.

When working over concrete hold carpet with clean concrete nails. No stay tack is used.

Because of the difference in carpet thickness, tackless strips cannot be installed a specified distance from the wall. Always use a piece of carpet in position shown, Illus. 89, to determine the proper distance tackless should be nailed. Hold the carpet scrap with backing against the wall. Slide a tackless strip with pins pointing to wall into pile. When carpet yarn covers the first row of pins, draw a line on floor to indicate edge of tackless. Do this at a number of points along each wall to make certain you allow proper size gully between wall and tackless. Draw lines and nail tackless in position required. This procedure is not used with shag or carpets of similar construction.

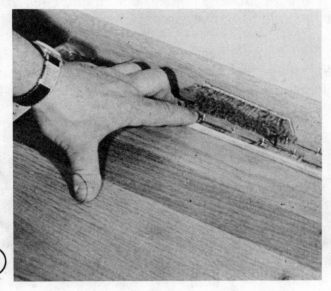

Installing tackless on a concrete floor with nails is not recommended where floors are subject to a moisture problem. Every nail driven into concrete accentuates the negative. Before driving nails into a concrete slab make certain there are no copper water or heating pipes buried in floor. See page 134 for information that explains how to bond tackless to concrete with adhesive.

Illus. 84 shows a proposed starting corner. The tackless strips have been securely fastened in place. To begin, position the carpet in starting corner, Illus. 85.

The carpet is fastened to approximately three feet of tackless in each direction. Use the kicker and a spreader, Illus. 36, to kick carpet onto tackless in corner.

When hooking the carpet into starting corner, place the kicker, Illus. 37, approximately 1½" from wall. At this point you are not stretching the carpet. You are just moving it forward. When carpet moves back after the kick, the angled pins in the tackless hooks into backing.

There are no teeth on the front 1" of this kicker. This permits kicker to ride over tackless forcing carpet into pins. To double check, rub hammer head over carpet.

The teeth in kicker grip carpet. The dial on this kicker, Illus. 90, permits adjusting the teeth so they don't go through the carpeting into the floor or concrete.

(90)

60

By setting the teeth to the exact height your carpet requires, Illus. 91, the kicker can be used to position carpet against tackless strip. Use the kicker to eliminate wrinkles. If teeth on kicker are set too deep, the teeth penetrate carpet and pull pad onto tackless. The teeth can also be burred or broken if forced into concrete. If teeth length is short, the kicker can slide across the face of the carpet and destroy the pile yarn.

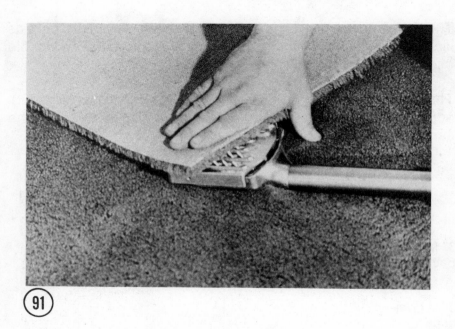

(91)

Most kickers also have a length adjustment. Set the tool to length convenient to you. The tool illustrated has a special safety shield that can be locked to protect teeth when not in use.

With 3' of carpet fastened to the tackless in corner AB, use the carpet stretcher, Illus. 25, 92, 93. The stretcher simplifies making a tight and straight installation. The one illustrated can be used in space as little as 33". It comes with extension poles that permit its use up to 22'.

(92)

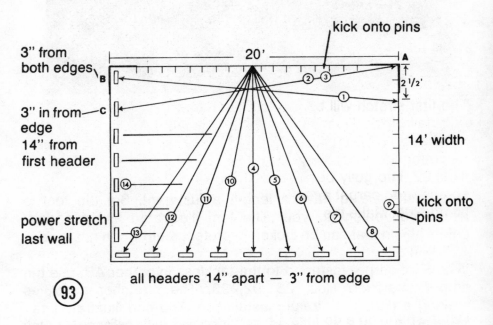

kick onto pins

3" from
both edges

20'

A

B

2½'

3" in from—c
edge
14" from
first header

1

14' width

4

10

5

14

kick onto
pins

power stretch
last wall

11

12

6

9

13

7

8

2

3

all headers 14" apart — 3" from edge

(93)

Install carpet net to a wood door saddle.

62

The teeth on a stretcher head, Illus. 94, must be adjusted to proper depth. The stretcher shown has an adjustment bar that raises and lowers the teeth. Ask your carpet retailer to demonstrate how deep the teeth should penetrate the carpet you purchase.

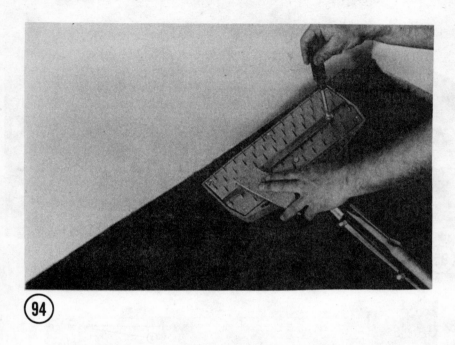

The first stretch will be the length of the room, Illus. 93, 95, 96. With tail block, Illus. 26, about 2½' from corner, and stretcher head about 4" from tackless strip. Stretch carpet amount retailer recommends. With stretcher holding carpet, press the spreader, Illus. 92, into gully between tackless strip and baseboard. Hold spreader on carpet and slowly release stretcher. The carpet will be hooked. Make the second stretch in position shown, Illus. 93.

The straight side or starting wall has been stretched. The next step (3), Illus. 93, is to kick the carpet onto the pins, along wall A, Illus. 96.

When spanning a doorway, Illus. 97, or archway, use a stay tack to hold carpet in position while you stretch it.

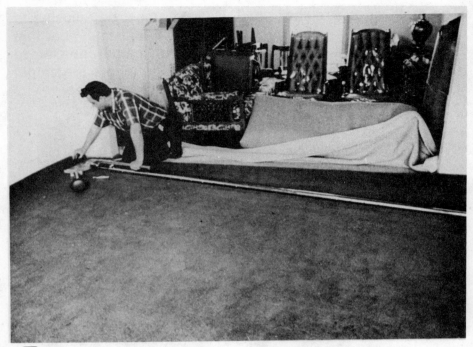

95

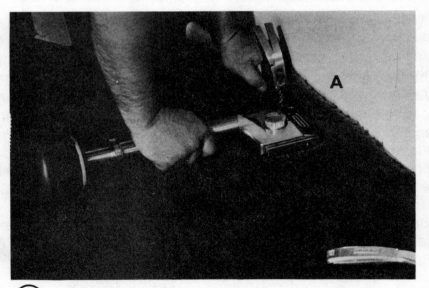

A

96

64

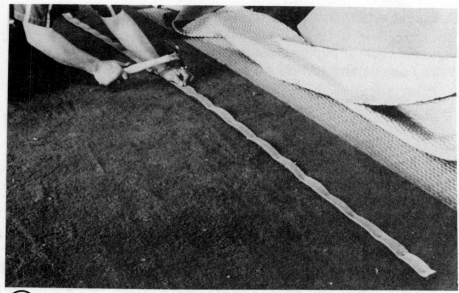

A stay tack can be any 2" or wider strip of carpet by any length available. Use it and 24 oz. tacks to hold carpet temporarily in position.

The first width stretch, (4), Illus. 93, 98, will be at center. After making the center stretch, the stretcher is repositioned a stretcher head apart and stretched at 5, 6, 7, 8, following schedule noted, Illus. 93. At this point, again use the kicker and kick carpet onto pins (9).

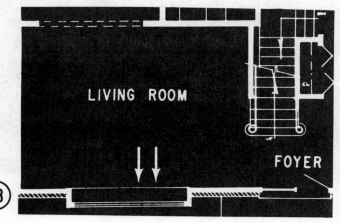

LIVING ROOM

FOYER

Using the stretcher, start at 10 and stretch at 11, 12, 13.

Power stretch straight across room (14). Power stretch the last wall by positioning stretcher a stretcher head apart, Illus. 99.

(99)

When fitting around steps and other obstructions, always stretch the carpet, Illus. 100, before making any cuts. A series of close relief cuts will allow the carpet to lay flat around obstruction.

(100)

The metal moulding required to finish an edge is always installed prior to installing carpet. No moulding is needed when installing matching carpet through a doorway or arch to an adjoining room. When fitting carpet to a metal moulding, Illus. 101, rough trim the carpet leaving about 1½" excess. Note mouldings shown on pages 137, 138.

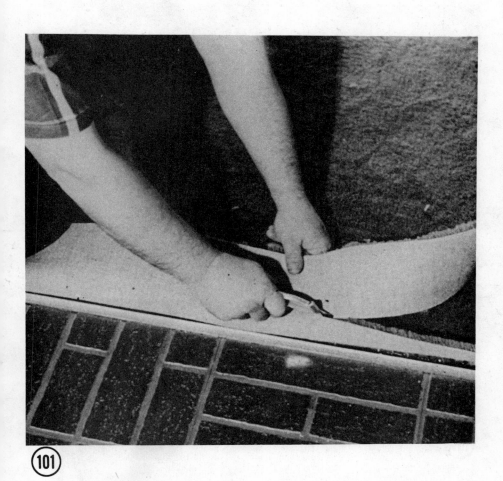

(101)

When laying conventional back carpet, kick the carpet to the moulding, Illus. 102, and chisel it under the lip. The two rows of teeth are on different angles. When the carpet is chiseled under the lip, the row of teeth closest to the lip penetrates the carpet backing. When the kicker is released and the carpet moves back, the last row of teeth also penetrate the backing.

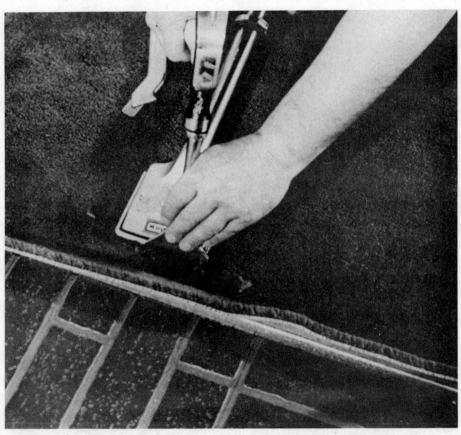

(102)

The trimmer, Illus. 28, used to trim conventional back carpeting, has two cutting adjustments, Illus. 103. The throat adjustment has three positions that accepts three different thicknesses of carpet. The two vertical walls of the trimmer hold the carpet in position for the blade.

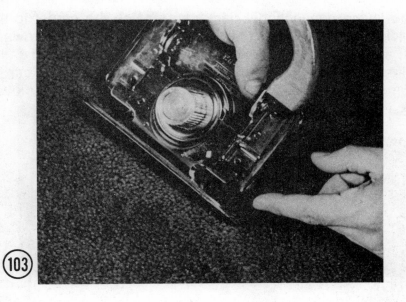

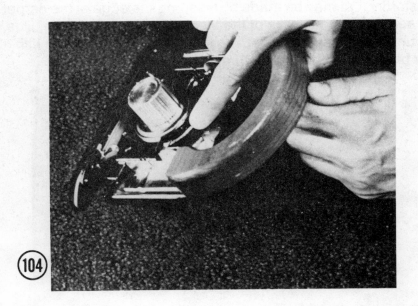

The outrigger holds cutting blades. Adjust the outrigger up or down determines how much carpet will be left at wall, Illus. 104. The outrigger tucks the excess carpet into the gully between the tackless strip and baseboard, Illus. 105.

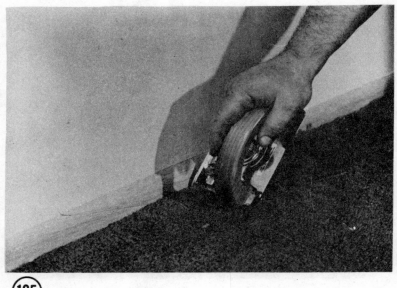

(105)

The starting cut may be made by inserting the edge of the carpet between the vertical walls of the trimmer and cutting down, Illus. 106, until base plate rests flat. Or the first cut can be made with a razor blade knife, then insert trimmer in cut.

(106)

To play safe, make first cut heavy. Push the trimmer forward and always towards the wall. The base plate must always rest flat on the floor, Illus. 107.

(107)

To cut the exact amount of carpet necessary to fit under lip of moulding, lay the knife blade flat on the metal lip, Illus. 108, and cut through the carpet backing.

(108)

Rub the excess carpet under the lip with a stair tool, Illus. 109.

(109)

The metal moulding lip is then hammered down flat with a rubber mallet or a 2 x 4 block and a hammer, Illus. 110.

(110)

Always cut, fit and nail tackless around a projection with the same gully spacing used along a wall, Illus. 111. Always nail each piece, regardless of size, with at least two nails. Carpet exerts a great pull on the strip so it must be securely fastened.

(111)

When tackless is installed against a starter step, or spindles, allow the same gully, and use two nails to secure each small piece, Illus. 112.

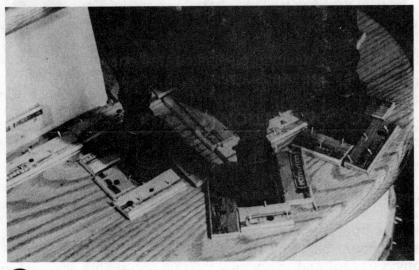

(112)

By installing an edge gripper moulding, Illus. 113, the carpet installed parallel to spindles, Illus. 114, will have a finished edge.

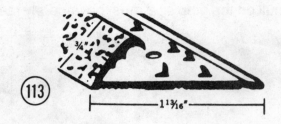

Where carpet meets a hard surface floor covering, Illus. 115, a metal, gripper bar, Illus. 116, is nailed in position to eliminate a tripping hazard and to conceal the raw edge. This also protects edge of carpet from water and wax used on the hard surface.

FASHION FINISH COLORS
  Antique Black
  Medium Green
  Sarasota Green
  Flame Red
  Royal Blue

|← 1⅝" →|

SEAMING CONVENTIONAL BACK

After first breadth has been fastened to tackless, and with factory edge, Illus. 117, trimmed off, fasten free edge with a stay tack in position noted.

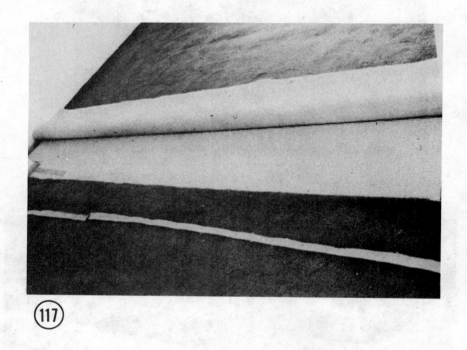

(117)

A stay tack can be any 2", or wider strip of carpet, by any length available. Use it and 24 oz. tacks to hold carpet temporarily in position.

Before cutting adjoining breadth, open it up and position it alongside to check the sweep on both pieces.

Next fold breadth over, Illus. 118. Using a chalk line, Illus. 30, snap a line approximately 1½" from factory edge.

Using a razor blade knife, Illus. 119, and a straight edge, Illus. 31, cut through the backing, Illus. 120. Do not kneel on fold.

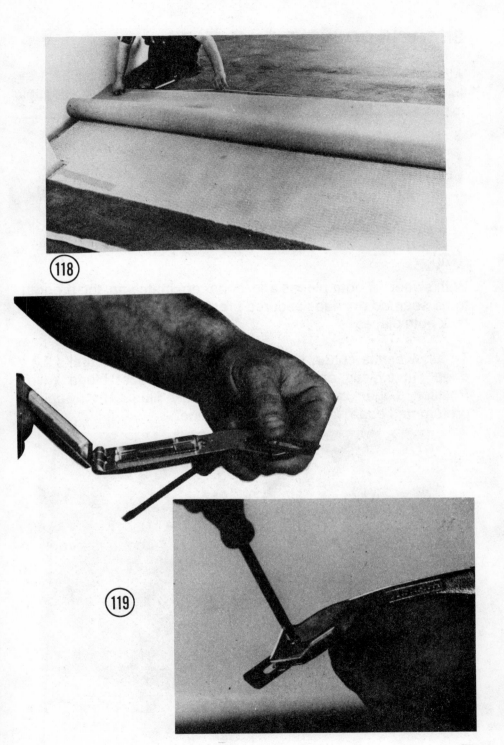

118

119

(120)

With sweep of both pieces and/or pattern matching, the breadth to be seamed overlaps secured breadth 1½". To play safe, stay tack both pieces.

To allow scribe cutter, Illus. 23, to make a trace cut, make a 1" deep cut exactly on seam line using the razor blade knife. Position finger guide of scribe cutter, Illus. 121, against pretrimmed edge. A matching cut is made.

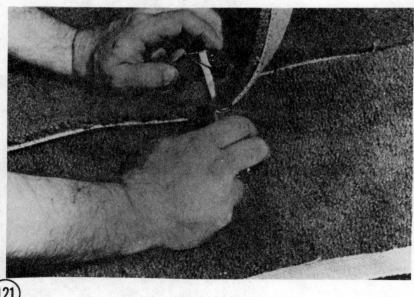

(121)

To set scribe cutter, loosen adjusting bar screw A, Illus. 121. Move bar until blades touch inside of lip B. Tighten screw A. Loosen throat adjustment screws C. Open or close throat to allow surplus edge to pass through throat. Keep finger on guide bar against finished edge as you pull scribe cutter toward you.

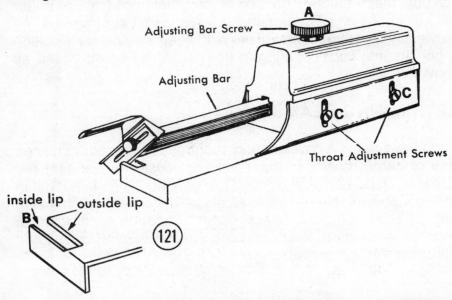

A
Adjusting Bar Screw

Adjusting Bar

C

C
Throat Adjustment Screws

inside lip   outside lip
B

(121)

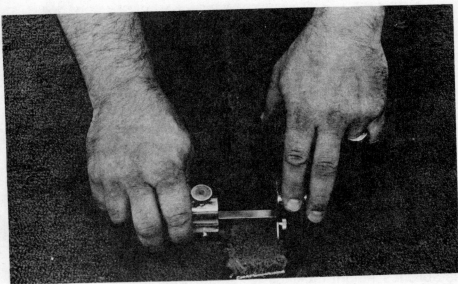

(121)

TO SCRIBE ALLOWING ¼" HEAVY

To cut free form shapes or to scribe an edge to meet a hard surface floor covering, you will want to cut heavy. Overlap carpet approximately 1½" to 2". Loosen adjustment bar screw A. Move bar until blade touches outside of lip. In this position the cutter will cut ¼" heavy. This means ¼" over exact cut required. As previously mentioned, first make a 1" deep starting cut. Position finger against floor covering to be scribed to, and proceed as above.

RETRIMMING SEAMS

If you have to cut a new seam, or reshape one already cut, keep face of carpet down. In this case you loosen adjustment bar screw A, Illus. 121, and remove bar from housing. Insert bar in position shown, Illus. 122. Set blade distance from housing surplus edge requires. Exact amount depends on amount of edge to be trimmed. Place housing against edge of carpet and pull cutter through carpet.

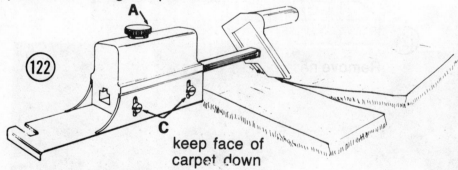

keep face of
carpet down

CARPETING STAIRS

Installing tackless on stairs follows this procedure. Nail tackless on riser, Illus. 123, before installing on tread.

To space tackless on riser, make a gauge. Cut four 2" pieces of tackless. Tape together, pin to pin, Illus. 124. This gauge establishes height tackless is nailed to riser from tread, Illus. 125. Rest tackless on gauge and nail to riser.

Remove nails, assemble gauge as shown.

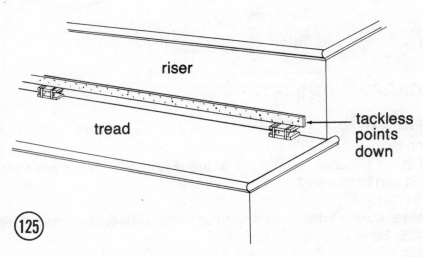

riser

tread

tackless
points
down

81

Tackless nailed to riser is cut 4" less in overall length of riser. This allows 2" on each side, Illus. 126.

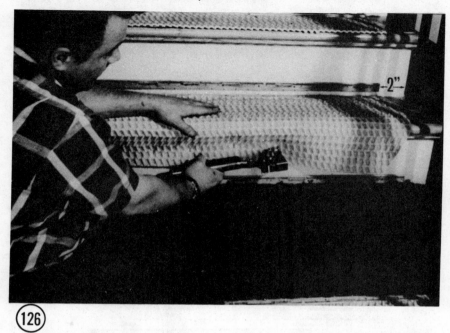

(126)

Nail the tackless to tread ¾" from riser, Illus. 127, or ½" from riser tackless.

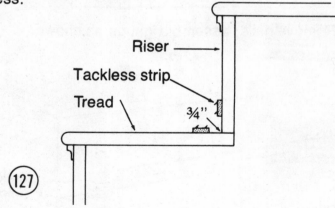

Riser ————

Tackless strip

Tread

¾"

(127)

Fasten tackless to floor the same distance from bottom riser as you did from a wall.

Always cut padding on a hard surface. Use carpet shears, Illus. 128, 24.

(128)

(129)

There are two accepted methods of padding stairs. You can use a single pad, Illus. 129, or to achieve a "pillowing" effect, use two layers, Illus. 130.

(130)

Cut the first pad to size that permits it to be stapled 1" from tackless. Staple to tread in 3 or 4 places, Illus. 131. The first pad is cut to fit flush with nose of tread. By keeping the first layer ¾" from tackless, the second layer can be stapled to tread without stapling through first pad.

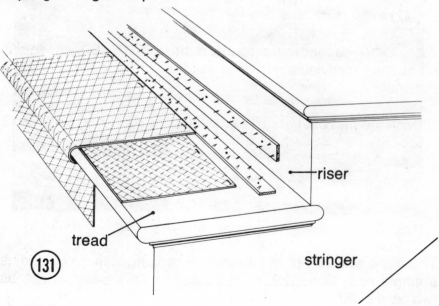

riser

tread

(131)

stringer

Cut the second layer of pad so it butts to edge of tackless and is wide enough to reach the center of the riser, Illus. 132. This piece should be cut so ends Vee in as shown, Illus. 133. This Vee in pad permits turning ends of carpet under so it lays flat on riser. Stretch this pad tight by hand.

(132)

Staple the second pad to bare tread in one inch spacing mentioned previously. These staples only go through the second layer.

Stretch the pad over nose of tread and staple to riser, Illus. 133.

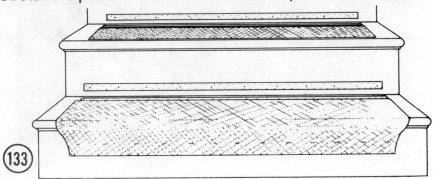

(133)

Cut a separate piece of carpet for the starting step about 4"
longer than tread. This allows a two inch turn on each end, Illus.
134.

(134)

Fasten carpet net to riser tackless, and take the first stretch at
center of step.

Fasten carpet to riser tackless to within 8" of both ends, Illus.
135.

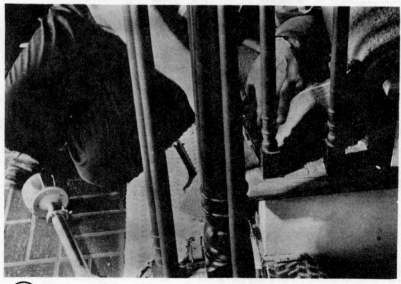

(135)

(136)

Make cuts to allow carpet to drop through spindles, Illus. 136.

Using the kicker, make the final stretch. You can now more accurately fit carpet to spindles, Illus. 137.

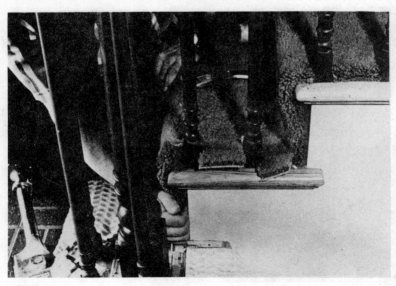

(137)

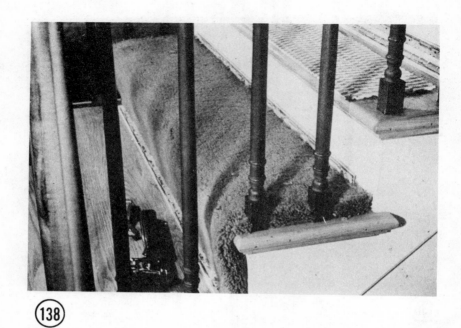

Turn excess carpet under to meet pad, Illus. 138.

There are two methods to hold carpet around a spindle. You can spread the pile yarn and drive a 14 oz. tack, or staple, Illus. 139.

(140)

The carpet at riser can be trimmed leaving about ½ to ¾ excess, Illus. 140. This excess is chiseled into the tackless gully. When done properly it's almost impossible to tell whether the stairs were carpeted with one, two or more pieces, Illus. 141.

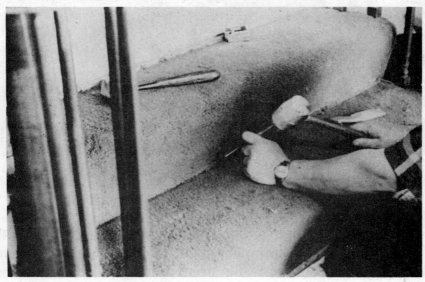

(141)

A single or double bird cage stairway, Illus. 142, requires a bit of skill. The easiest way to get practice is to use some old carpeting, or cut a paper pattern. Get a roll of heavy building paper and assume it's carpeting that can't be stretched. Go through all the step-by-step procedures. If any step stops you, ask your carpet retailer to clarify same before cutting carpeting.

(142)

Stairs can have a single or double bird cage. To ascertain width of carpet the starting step will require, run a fabric tape measure across the widest point of the tread from the floor, behind the step, through the bird cage across the tread, to floor. Add 4", Illus. 143.

90

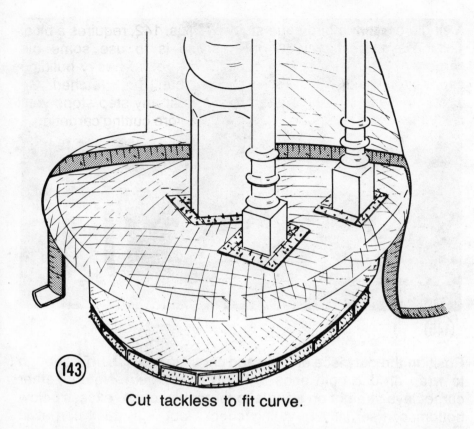

(143)

Cut tackless to fit curve.

To ascertain length needed, place end of tape on stringer, Illus. 144, 145 around nose, to other stringer. Add 4".

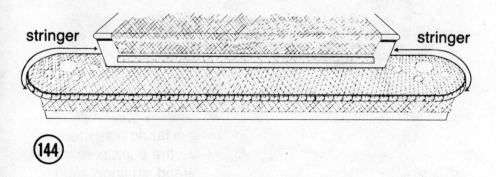

stringer   stringer

(144)

Position the cut piece on step and check to see if there's enough to wrap around both ends to finish at stringers. Note whether carpet lays straight on tread and there is about 4" excess below bottom of riser. If everything checks out, stay tack carpet in place at center of step, Illus. 146.

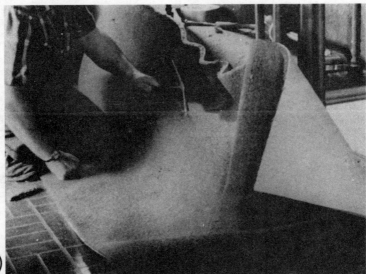

(146)

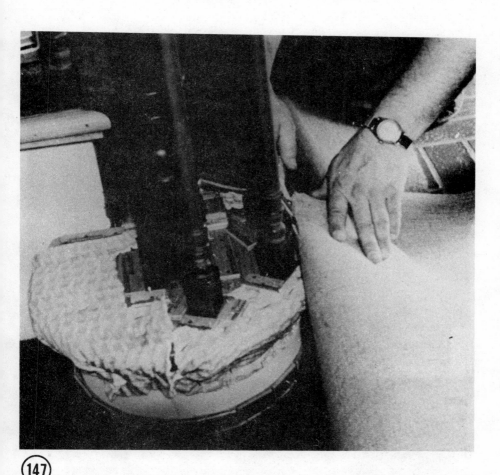

Before marking the cap, wrap carpet around spindles, Illus. 147. The first cut is made from riser to center of first spindle, Illus. 148.

Position carpet alongside next spindle and cut from center of spindle to depth required, Illus. 148. Use extreme care in making cuts as the circular piece of carpet being cut fits inside the bird cage when these cut pieces are refitted in position. You can now appreciate why this step requires practice before using the finished carpeting.

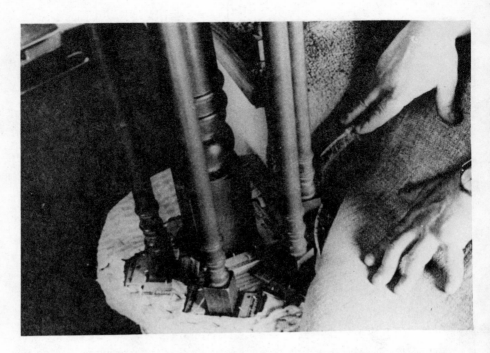

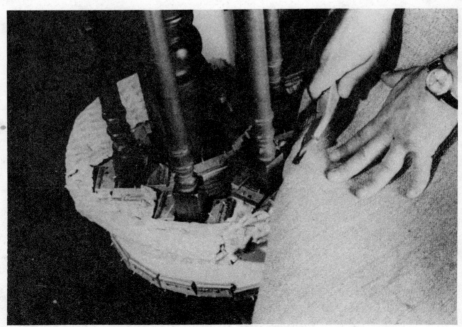

When cuts have been made to center of each spindle, and with all tail ends left in place, fit carpet into bird cage, Illus. 149, 150.

(150)

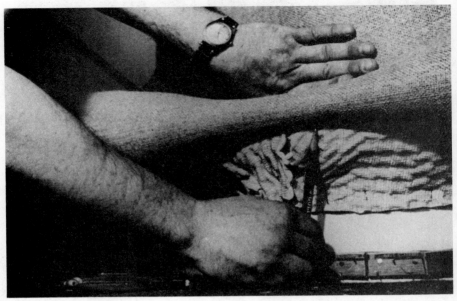

(151)

You are now ready to mark outline of cap. Hold a pencil against nose of step, Illus. 151, and trace outline of step. Be sure to hold pencil vertical.

Pull the carpet back on the step so it lays reasonable flat. Place a piece of plywood on padding, and using a knife, don't use shears, cut along drawn line, Illus. 152.

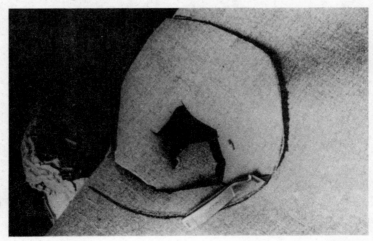

(152)

(153)

The tread cut is now in position, Illus. 153.

The riser carpet must now be wrapped around the riser, stringer to stringer. Make a series of short relief cuts to permit carpet to wrap smoothly around riser, Illus. 154.

(154)

(155)

Press carpet against riser and trace outline of nose, Illus. 155. Trim excess carpet above the tread.

Illus. 156 shows progress to this point. Note riser is reasonably even and the seam falls just over the nose.

(156)

Using a single 18 oz. waxed linen thread, and a 1¾ or 2" needle, sew a cross joint stitch and pull thread tight, Illus. 157. If you don't know how to sew carpet, ask your carpet retailer.

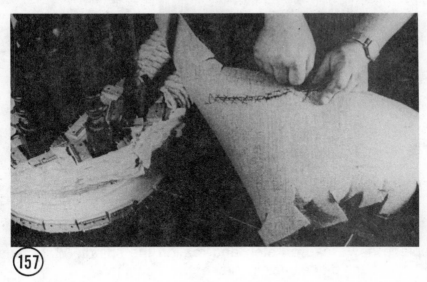

(157)

Use latex to vulcanize the seam and to keep the seam from "grinning", Illus. 158. Follow manufacturer's directions and allow latex to set up before moving. Use a scrap piece of carpet to spread latex over seam.

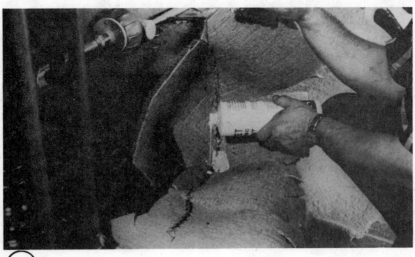

(158)

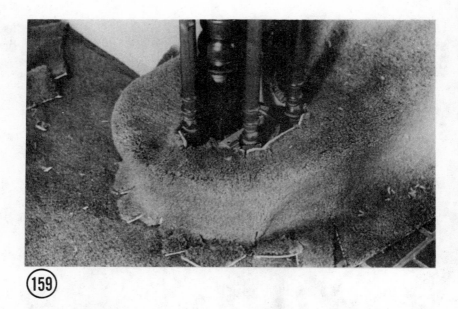

(159)

Replace sewn cap on step and realign the spindle cuts, Illus. 159. Get each piece back in their original position.

If necessary, use a kicker, Illus. 160, to move carpet to line up original cuts. Use the kicker to spread and lock carpet in position.

(160)

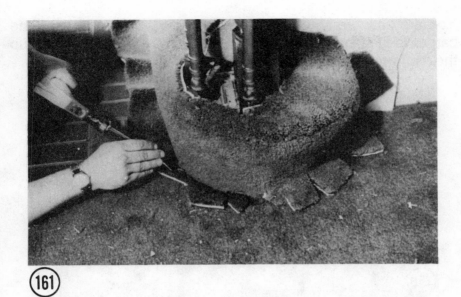

(161)

Rub carpet onto tackless around spindles, Illus. 161. Chisel the carpet onto tackless at floor. This stretches carpet down riser.

After carpet has been hooked onto riser tackless and stretched onto tackless around spindles, the cap is locked into place, Illus. 162.

(162)

You are now ready to fit carpet to spindles, Illus. 163. Nick the carpet to fit spindle. Use an awl to stretch any excess carpet up the riser and into the bird cage.

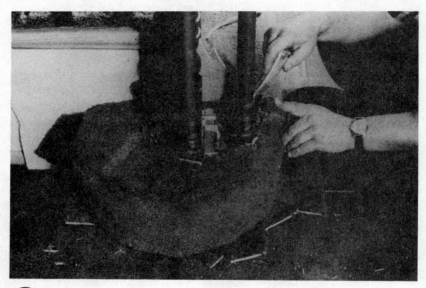

(163)

(164)

Apply seam sealer to original cuts and put carpet back together in bird cage, or use tacks or staples. The carpet on inside of bird cage must be tacked or stapled in position so a vacuum cleaner or whisk broom doesn't lift the carpet or pull tufts from any raw edge, Illus. 164.

Remove the stay tack from center of tread, Illus. 165. Using a kicker stretch carpet on an angle to the opposite side of the step and tack with a concealed tack.

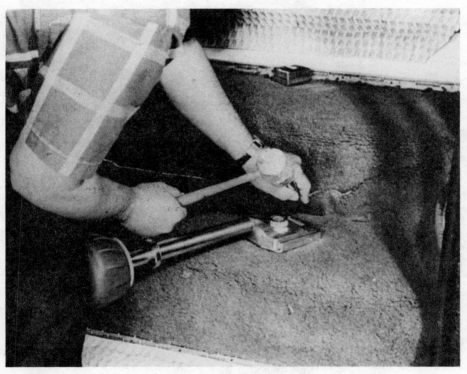

(165)

A completed cap, Illus. 166, should show no raw edges. The two layers of padding have not altered the step. The carpet on riser has been folded under and tacked in place.

Always cut carpeting on upper hall floor wide enough to cover top riser, Illus. 167.

WET OR LATEX SEAM—CONVENTIONAL BACK

After both seam edges have been cut and dry fit, a latex seam is made in the following way.

Cut a length of 4" wide paper backed face seaming tape to length seam requires. Hook one end on tackless in position so it centers tape under seam, Illus. 168. Stretch it tight under stay tacked edge.

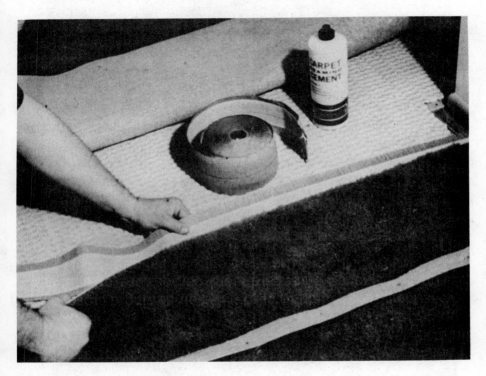

(168)

As previously mentioned, the yarn lays down in one direction and stands up in the opposite direction. This is called sweep. The seam edge that sweeps away from the seam is set into the cement first. This prevents face yarn from overlapping seam.

Using latex cement, seal raw carpet edge . Apply latex to back at base of yarn, Illus. 169. Use a piece of carpet as a brush.

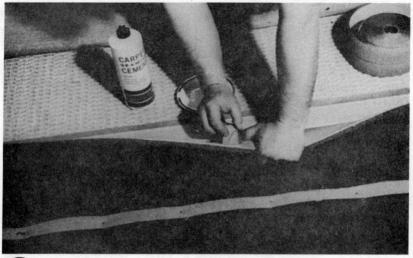

(169)

Next pour the latex seaming cement on the seaming tape and spread it with "brush", Illus. 170. Use enough latex to fill fiberglass webbing but not enough to bleed through carpet seam. Don't allow cement to ooze over onto pad.

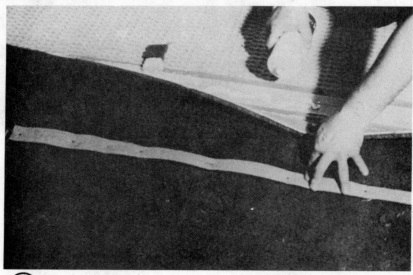

(170)

If the seam is 15 feet or less, you can spread latex over entire tape. If over 15 feet, do the seam in stages, Illus. 171. Since this cement sets up fast when spread thin, position the backing onto the tape as fast as possible.

Always fit latex seams, hand sewn seams or cushion back seams at center first, then work toward the end.

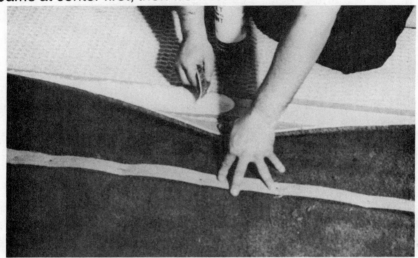

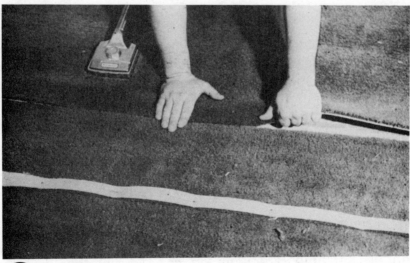

Fit seams on the heavy side to make certain backings are tight, Illus. 172.

A cross joint adds length to carpet. When sewing a cross joint, position both pieces on a cardboard carpet core or stretcher handle, Illus. 173, to keep the seam edge as flat as possible.

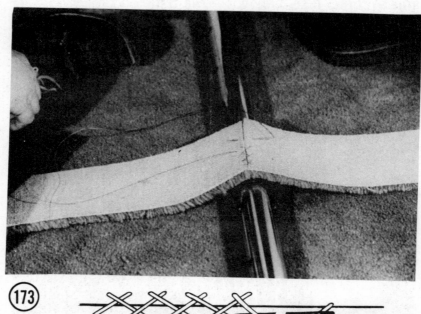

Sew cross joint stitch, Illus. 173, using a single, 18 ox. waxed linen carpet thread, and a 1¾ or 2" needle. Alternate the stitch so the needle doesn't penetrate the backing in a straight line.

Use overcast stitch, Illus. 174, when adding width to a carpet. Use a double thread.

Reinforce sewn seams with latex seaming cement, Illus. 175. Pour the latex onto an area away from the seam.

Using carpet scrap, spread cement across seam and rub it into backing, Illus. 176. Overlap seam 1½" on both sides. Allow cement to set time directions on can advise, then position carpet.

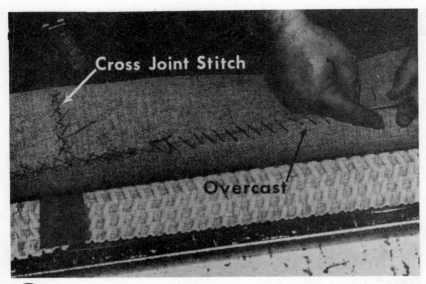

Cross Joint Stitch

Overcast

(174)

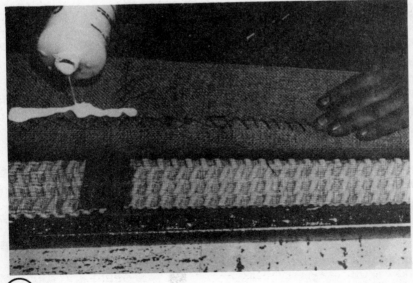

(175)

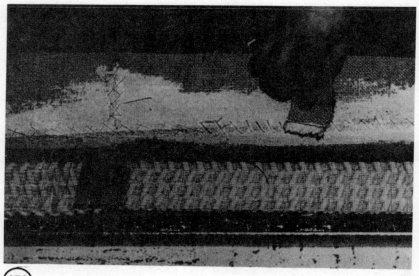

(176)

Always stay tack a wet seam in position. Allow seam to dry before removing stay tacks. When stretching, the stay tack protects the seam.

HOT MELT SEAMING

For those who want to make carpeting a career, hot melt seaming provides a quick, effective method of seaming conventional back carpet. Don't practice hot melt seaming on a job. Practice with scrap.

Some important points to remember:

1. Be sure adhesive is completely melted before applying iron. A "false" or part melt prevents adhesive from penetrating into carpet and tape.

2. Excessive iron heat can penetrate and distort face fibers causing discoloration and alter pile-lay over seam area.

3. Since most primary and secondary carpet backings differ in their ability to absorb heat, it's important to test hot melt seaming on each quality of carpet, prior to the actual installation.

110

(177)

Since some types of carpet permit face cutting, use the seam cutter, Illus. 177, to separate the rows of yarn. This permits face cutting. As previously mentioned, since this cuts close to one side, cut one edge in one direction, the other in opposite direction, Illus. 178.

(178)

The iron, edge seaming cement, and tape, Illus. 179, are the basic tools required for making hot melt tape seams. In many installations, you will also need the kicker and sometimes a stretcher.

(179)

Use extreme care when you make a hot seam. If you are doing the work on a floor that isn't to be covered with carpeting, protect it with hardboard, Illus. 180.

(180)

Fasten the end of hot melt seam tape by hooking it onto the tackless. If working away from the area to be carpeted, tape or tack the tape in position to hold both ends, Illus. 181.

(181)

After trimming edges and testing to make certain they fit dry, Illus. 182, place the hot melt seam tape down center of seam, then stretch both breadths lengthwise and stay tack to hold in place.

(182)

Seal edges with carpet seaming cement to lock in edge rows of pile, Illus. 183. Edge seaming retards delamination of secondary backing. Use a scrap piece of carpet to apply edge cement.

(183)

When sealing iron is heated to temperature iron specifies, place iron on tape until adhesive in tape has melted, Illus. 181. Keep edge of carpet away from iron.

Since the adhesive cools rapidly, you have to move the iron, press the carpet into the hot tape, Illus. 184, and rub it lightly with the flat of your hand, Illus. 185, while the iron is melting the next section of tape.

Hot melt adhesive dries hard so avoid excessive pressure on the carpet with your hands or tools. This caution is especially important when seaming over padding. Surface depressions will remain in carpet after adhesive sets.

114

(184)

(185)

115

The iron should be moved through the seam at a rate of approximately three to four feet per minute. After making the seam, leave it undisturbed for 5 to 8 minutes, or until the seam is cool, Illus. 186.

(186)

When seaming large sections, and/or pattern material, stay tack the ends, Illus. 187, about one foot on each side of a seam to keep carpet in position and the seam flat.

The slight tension along the seam edge keeps seams in position. Whenever possible make all long seams over a bare floor before installing a pad, Illus. 188.

PLEASE NOTE: In developing this book the author selected and illustrated tools popular with the carpet installers. Since manufacturers continually make design changes which, in many cases, alter the use of a specific tool, it's important to double check the end use of each rental tool with the dealer. Since he will know what step of the work you want to accomplish, he can tell you how to use the tool.

(187)

(188)

117

WHERE TO USE MOULDINGS

The special mouldings shown on pages 137,138,simplify solving most installations. All are predrilled and are secured to floor with nails. Always snap chalk lines and install moulding to the line.

When a hinged door separates two rooms where one floor is carpeted with conventional back, and the other cushion back, Illus. 76, a T-shaped moulding, Illus. 77, is installed. The cushion back is again secured with adhesive, the conventional back with pins. Both lips are hammered down using the rubber mallet.

The binder bar, Illus. 78, can be installed between two rooms separated by a sliding door, Illus. 79.

To cut the exact amount of carpet necessary to fit under the lip, angle the razor blade knife, Illus.189, against the metal lip. Cut carpet. After both lips have been hammered down (use the rubber mallet), you have a master crafted installation.

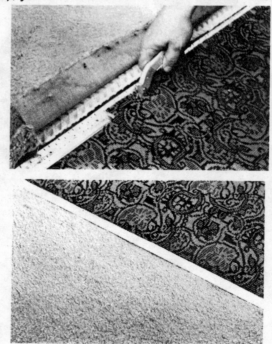

(189)

118

When conventional back carpet meets a hard surface floor, the metal gripper bar, Illus. 115, 116, is used. Stretch carpet onto pins, then hammer down edge over carpet.

Always use a miter box, Illus. 190, and a hacksaw to cut mouldings.

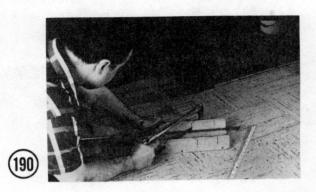

(190)

Before cutting an inside or outside corner, it's necessary to first tap down the lip with a mallet or block of wood, Illus. 191.

(191)

After cutting the miter, fit the pieces together, Illus. 192. When using some mouldings it's necessary to cut away part of the underslung section to achieve a tight corner. Use metal snips.

(192)

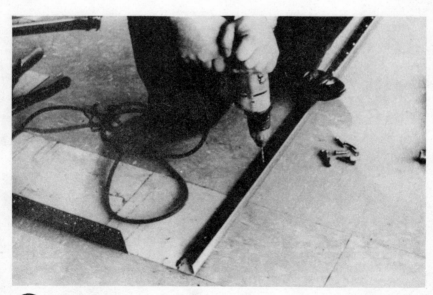

(193)

On wood floors, fasten moulding at miter end first. On concrete floors drill a hole through metal into concrete about a foot from miter end. Since the moulding is predrilled, knick the concrete with a center punch to keep the carbide tipped drill bit from traveling. Hold metal with your feet, Illus. 193, while drilling.

Always drill holes slightly deeper than length of nail used. Use a 3/16 carbide tipped drill bit and 1¼" sinker nail. The diameter of the nail is slightly larger than the hole drilled, Illus. 194. Drive nails in at miter end last when fastening moulding to concrete. Drive all nails so heads finish flush.

194

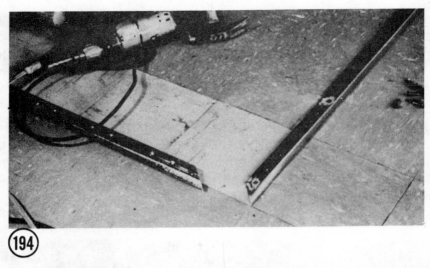

(194)

After securing moulding, raise lip to receive carpet, then tap lip down tight to floor.

One way to make a tight miter when fastening moulding to a concrete floor is to angle drill towards the piece already fastened, Illus. 195. When you drive the nail, it forces moulding into corner.

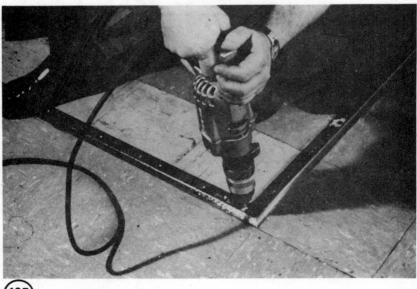

(195)

When mitered corners are securely fastened, drive a nail at center and another at other end. Then drill and nail every 6".

Illus. 195, 197, shows the type of moulding used with conventional back carpet when no padding is to be installed. This moulding can be fastened to concrete by drilling ⅛" holes with a carbide tipped drill bit, then nailing with ¾" concrete nails.

Illus. 196, shows various shapes used, conventional back carpet (with teeth), glue down carpet (no teeth).

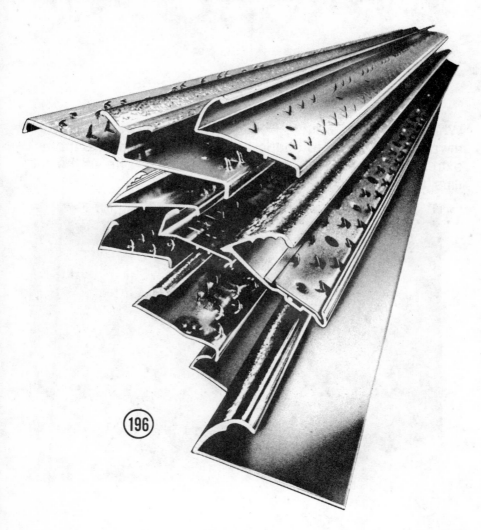

(197)

When installing flex trim, Illus. 198, or slotted metal, Illus. 199, always bend metal to shape by hand. If you have to make an extreme outside bend, use pliers to remove one of the tabs, Illus. 200, so they don't overlap.

(198)

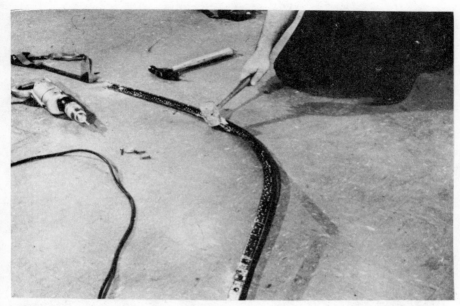

125

First fasten the metal at both ends of the bend, Illus. 201. When bending to an outside radius, the slotted tabs raise up. Hammer these down flat using a hammer and stair tool before drilling holes. Use care not to bend teeth.

(201)

Slotted metal can be hand bent to almost any shape required.

Always nail slotted metal at opposite ends, then drill and nail every hole in all the large tabs.

When fitting carpet to a metal shape, rough trim the carpet leaving about an 1½" overage, Illus. 101.

Kick the carpet to the moulding, Illus. 102, and chisel it under the lip. The row of teeth closest to the lip penetrate the backing. When the kicker is released the carpet moves back. The last row of teeth also penetrate the backing.

To cut carpet so edge fits under lip, lay the razor blade knife, Illus. 108, on the metal lip, and cut through the backing.

Rub the excess carpet under the lip with a stair tool, Illus. 109.

Hammer metal lip down using a rubber mallet, Illus. 110.

Always allow sufficient excess to lay over the moulding, Illus. 202. Always cut cushion back two or three rows of yarn heavy. This allows enough to fit under lip. Always install cushion back with adhesive on moulding. It's the adhesive that holds the carpet. The tap down lip only protects the cut edge.

(202)

SPECIAL SITUATIONS

Before installing cushion back carpet alongside spindles, Illus. 113, install moulding, Illus. 74, 1" or distance from spindles desired. When you spread adhesive, cover moulding up to lip, but don't allow it to build up under lip.

Since the spindles are too close to hold knife at an angle, cut the carpet heavy, i.e., with sufficient overage to allow carpet to cover lip, Illus. 113. Using the handle of a knife or stair tool, rub the carpet on top of the lip. When you pull the carpet back, you can see the line of the lip, Illus. 203. Cut carpet leaving lip line on carpet. This provides just the right excess to fit under lip. Press carpet back onto adhesive. Run an awl through to tuck any loose ends and hammer down lip.

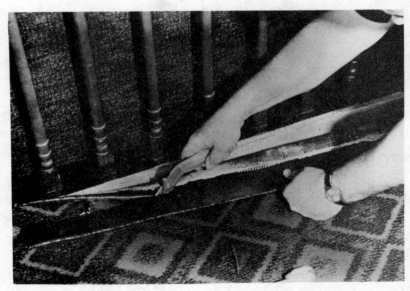

PATTERN MATCHING

When installing pattern, Illus. 204, cut each breadth with 4"
overage. Two inches at each end permits repositioning, when
necessary, to realign pattern. Before cutting the second and
succeeding breadths, roll each out, allow for excess. Match
pattern at center, then cut breadth.

Where any drops or fill-ins are required, make certain to allow
for same plus the 2". This permits wall trimmer to cut more
accurately.

To match a pattern it's necessary to cut selvage edge off both
breadths. Retract blade in seam cutter, Illus. 19. Run tool
through row of yarn selected, then repeat with blade extended,
Illus. 20.

Always dry fit a pattern to make certain it matches.

COVING CARPET

If you want to cove carpet 3", 4" or 6" up a wall or toe space,
allow for same when cutting each breadth. Cut each breadth
heavy so it extends just above cap. For a cushion back
installation, nail cap moulding, Illus. 74, 205, at height required.

Snap a chalk line and nail metal cove to line.
Cut pieces of 1 x 2 to length needed to rest
cove at height required.

Crease carpet at floor, Illus. 82. Rest the razor blade knife on top of cap moulding, Illus. 206, and cut excess. Press carpet into cap. Run an awl through to tuck in any loose ends.

If you are running carpet up a wall with an outside or inside corner, Illus. 207, it's much easier to cut separate pieces to width and length required. A separate piece can be embedded in adhesive without any need to cut triangles, etc.

TO PROTECT YOUR HOME
INSTALL UNDER CARPET ALARM MATS

Today's way of life requires installation of as much protection as you and your home can afford. Complete details for the installation of a complete electronic alarm system is explained in Book #695, see page 146. Step-by-step directions suggest installing under the carpet surveillance alarm mats, Illus. 208, 209, 210, 211. These paper thin mats should be placed across an area adjacent to an entry door, at the base of stairs, in a foyer, or any area an intruder may normally penetrate. Use doublefaced tape to fasten in position. Do not staple. Connect wires from one mat to another, then to protective alarm circuit. A concealed switch can activate or deactivate the mats when the perimeter house circuit is activated. Book #696 provides complete details. These mats are installed before padding and carpeting. Always lay #15 felt over a concrete floor before installing carpet mat alarms.

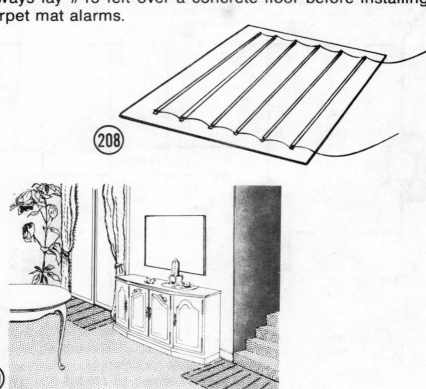

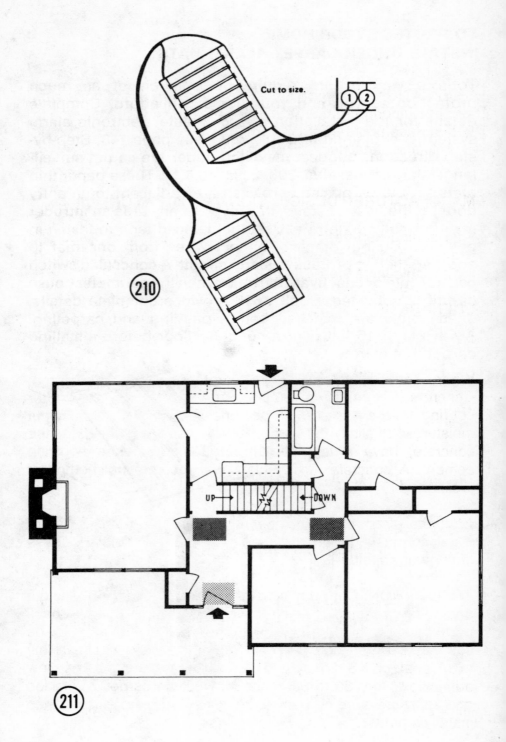

Cut to size.

① ②

210

UP→ →DOWN

211

APPLICATION: To install all types of carpet padding, foam, hair, jute, sponge rubber, rubberized felt, polyurethane, etc., to hard surface floors—concrete, marble, wood, terrazzo, asphalt, vinyl tile and metal decking.

MANUFACTURER DESIGNATION: KS120 Pad Cement

Fast setting non-freezing, water resistant, colorless when dry. Prevents padding movement when stretching carpeting. Bonding strength increases with age.

PREPARATION: All subfloors, above or below grade, must be smooth, clean, level, form, dry and free of dust, dirt, wax, paint, grease and foreign matter. If in doubt as to finish, sand surface.

When applied to concrete, concrete must be fully cured. Concrete is normally considered cured 28 or more days after pouring unless affected by dampness, etc. If in doubt about moisture, alkalinity or hydrostatic pressure affecting the concrete, have a test of floor area made before applying cement. A concrete mixing plant can recommend method of testing.

Concrete floor must be thoroughly cured and dry before installing padding. It must not be subject to sweat or dampness during rainy spell.

APPLICATION: Cut padding to overall size needed and lay out dry. When trimmed to exact size required, fold 3" to 4" back from tackless strip, and also where two pieces are to be seamed. Using a scrap piece of carpet as a brush, spread a thin even coat of KS120 over 3" to 4" area around pad. Allow adhesive to dry 30 to 60 seconds. Replace carpet in position and apply pressure by walking on cemented area. You can then install carpet.

133

DANGER: KS120, like most of these cements and clean up solvents, is extremely flammable. The vapors can even cause a flash fire. Diconnect all electrical appliances. Keep area well ventiliated. Do not smoke or allow anyone to come into the area with a lighted cigarette. Be sure to extinguish all pilot lights, stoves, heaters, oil burners, etc. Ventilate area thoroughly after using and before using any appliances. Avoid prolonged breathing of vapors.

APPLICATION: To glue tackless carpet strip to plywood, concrete, terrazzo, tile, and other porous and non-porous surfaces.

MANUFACTURER DESIGNATION: KS110 Tackless Strip Cement

KS119 Clean-up Solvent

CHARACTERISTICS: Fast setting. Withstands normal carpet stretching after adhesive has been allowed to set time manufacturer specifies. Resistant to water, heat, oil. When applied as specified, bonding strength increases with age.

PREPARATION: All floor surfaces must be structurally sound, dry, free of dust, dirt, wax, paint, shellac, varnish, and other foreign matter. Sand area where tackless strip is to be applied. Wipe floor with a cloth dampened in KS119 solvent. Accurately position tackless distance from wall as shown, Illus. 89. Draw lines on floor to indicated tackless.

Stir adhesive thoroughly. Using a 2" roller, trowel, or brush, apply a thin coat of KS110 to floor where tackless is to be applied.

134

Cut tackless to 6" lengths when applying to concrete; 18" lengths over plywood, wood, terrazzo. Apply a thin coat of KS110 to tackless strip. Allow both to dry approximately 15 minutes. To test when dry, KS110 will not transfer to finger touch. Place tackless in position. Apply uniform pressure using a tapping block (2 x 4) and mallet.

CAUTION: Keep containers tightly sealed when not in use. Store in temperature between 40°F and 100°. If stored below 40°F, the cement will thicken. While this doesn't effect bond properties, the cement will only be workable when brought back to room temperature.

If cement thickens as a result of being left unsealed, discard same.

DANGER: This cement is extremely flammable. Keep away from open flame, sparks, excessive heat. Do not use in an area where there are any electric motors and appliances, fans, appliances, refrigerators, gas pilot lights, clocks, etc., in operation. Disconnect these before using this cement. Do not smoke or allow anyone else to come into the area when this cement is being used. Avoid prolonged breathing of vapor. Keep room well ventilated during application. Avoid contact with skin.

KEEP CONTAINER TIGHTLY CLOSED WHEN NOT IN USE.

COVERAGE: Approximately 1400 lineal feet of tackless strip can be bonded per quart (two surfaces).

AUTHOR'S NOTE: Due to variance and combination of ingredients, always follow directions manufacturer provides.

APPLICATION: To glue down jute, sponge, foam, polypro—pylene and neoprene backed, and indoor/outdoor carpeting.

MANUFACTURER DESIGNATION: KS 155 M — Multi–Purpose Adhesive.

CHARACTERISTIC: Non–flammable, alkali and water resistant and freeze-thaw stable may be used over suspended plywood and concrete floors, on grade or below grade.

PREPARATION: Store both carpeting and adhesive in a room with 70°F or higher temperature for at least 24 hours before installing. Keep room and especially floor surface at 70°F during installation, and for at least 24 hours after completion.

When applying to concrete, the floor must be fully cured and completely free of moisture, alkalinity and hydrostatic pressure.

Floor area must be smooth, clean, level, firm, dry and free of dust, dirt, wax, paint, grease, curing agents, and any foreign matter.

Stir adhesive and apply with a 3/32" x ⅛ x 3/32" notched trowel. Hold trowel at a 45° angle.

Use KS 150 seam sealer.

Coverage: 150 - 200 square yards per gallon.

ALUMINUM BINDER BARS & CARPET GRIPPERS

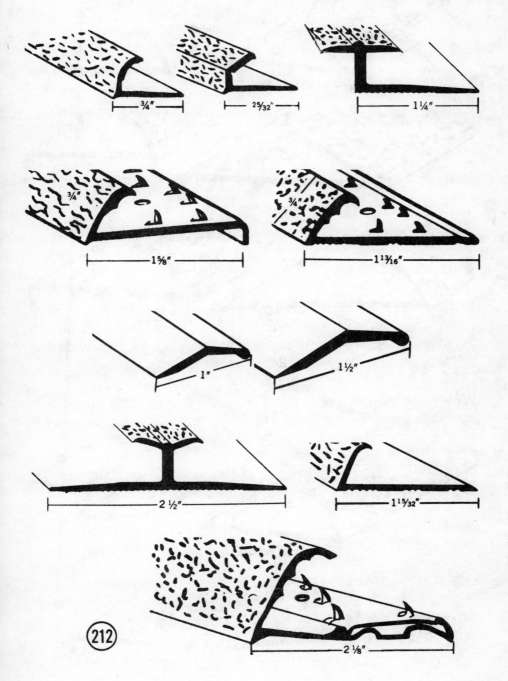

3/4"

2 5/32"

1 1/4"

3/4"   1 5/8"

3/4"   1 13/16"

1"   1 1/2"

2 1/2"

1 15/32"

212

2 1/8"

137

ALUMINUM BINDER BARS & CARPET GRIPPERS (continued)

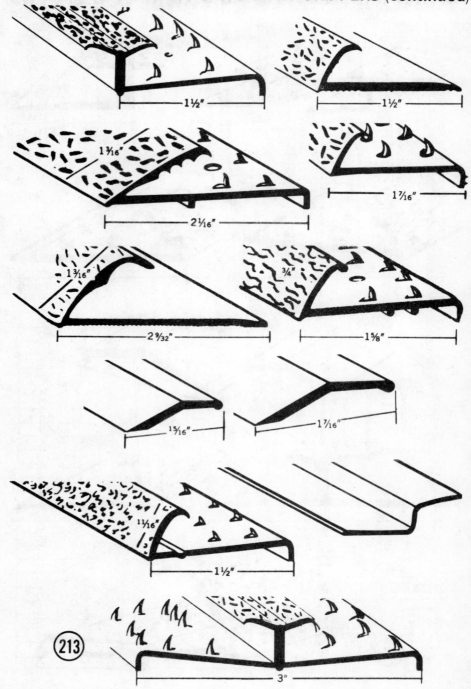

1½"

1½"

1³⁄₁₆"

2¹⁄₁₆"

1⁷⁄₁₆"

1³⁄₁₆"

2⁹⁄₃₂"

¾"

1⅝"

1⁵⁄₁₆"

1⁷⁄₁₆"

1¹⁄₁₆"

1½"

⑵⑬

3"

HANDY REFERENCE - NAILS

Common — Finishing —

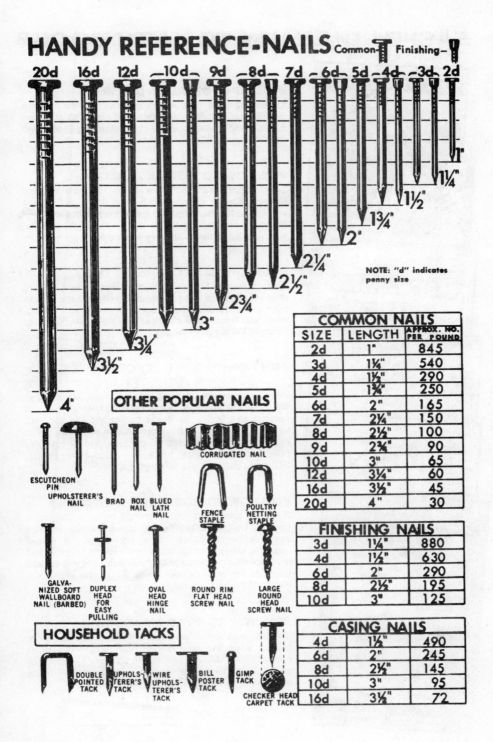

20d 16d 12d 10d 9d 8d 7d 6d 5d 4d 3d 2d

1"
1¼"
1½"
1¾"
2"
2¼"
2½"
2¾"
3"
3¼"
3½"
4"

NOTE: "d" indicates penny size

OTHER POPULAR NAILS

ESCUTCHEON PIN

UPHOLSTERER'S NAIL

BRAD

BOX NAIL

BLUED LATH NAIL

CORRUGATED NAIL

FENCE STAPLE

POULTRY NETTING STAPLE

GALVA-NIZED SOFT WALLBOARD NAIL (BARBED)

DUPLEX HEAD FOR EASY PULLING

OVAL HEAD HINGE NAIL

ROUND RIM FLAT HEAD SCREW NAIL

LARGE ROUND HEAD SCREW NAIL

HOUSEHOLD TACKS

DOUBLE POINTED TACK

UPHOLS-TERER'S TACK

WIRE UPHOLS-TERER'S TACK

BILL POSTER TACK

GIMP TACK

CHECKER HEAD CARPET TACK

COMMON NAILS

SIZE	LENGTH	APPROX. NO. PER POUND
2d	1"	845
3d	1¼"	540
4d	1½"	290
5d	1¾"	250
6d	2"	165
7d	2¼"	150
8d	2½"	100
9d	2¾"	90
10d	3"	65
12d	3¼"	60
16d	3½"	45
20d	4 "	30

FINISHING NAILS

3d	1¼"	880
4d	1½"	630
6d	2"	290
8d	2½"	195
10d	3"	125

CASING NAILS

4d	1½"	490
6d	2"	245
8d	2½"	145
10d	3"	95
16d	3½"	72

139

EASI-BILD® LEARN TO EARN BOOKS

#603 HOW TO BUILD A DORMER

Those who need more living space can raise a roof with a big dormer. Step-by-step directions take all the fear, mystery and inflated cost out of transforming an attic into liveable space. 82pp., 114 illus.

#605 HOW TO INSTALL PANELING

Learn to apply paneling like a pro. Build a matching wall to wall storage closet with sliding doors, a fireplace mantel, install valances with indirect lighting, even build a cedar lined storage room. 146pp., 214 illus., plus full size valance patterns simplify every step.

#606 HOW TO LAY CERAMIC TILE

Easy to follow, step-by-step directions explain how to prepare a floor or wall prior to laying ceramic tile, how to estimate material needed, cut and fit tile around tub, toilet, etc. Read, learn, then see how easily you can make ceramic tile repairs like a pro. 98pp., 137 illus.

#607 HOW TO BUILD FENCES, GATES OUTDOOR PROJECTS

Every homeowner who appreciates privacy recognizes the need for fencing. Six different styles of colonial fencing can easily be made by tracing the full size patterns contained in this book. It also simplifies building a colonial sign post, an outdoor display cabinet - bulletin board, canopy, trellis, and much more. 162pp., 212 illus., plus full size lettering pattern.

#608 HOW TO MODERNIZE A KITCHEN

Building base and wall cabinets, then installing a continuous countertop to size space permits, enables every reader to modernize a kitchen at the lowest possible cost. Besides providing needed storage and work space, a modernized kitchen adds a sizeable Capital Gains to the value of your home. Every step explained. 82pp., 118 illus.

#609 HOW TO BUILD AN ADDITION

Creating additional living space can prove to be one of today's soundest investments. Step-by-step directions explain how to build a 12 x 16', 16 x 24' or any other size one or two story addition, with or without an outside entry. 162pp., 211 illus., simplify every step.

140

#611 HOW TO BUILD
GREENHOUSES - SUNHOUSES

Enjoy the fun of gardening all winter in this energy saving walk-in greenhouse. When built adjacent to a basement door or window, it captures waste heat. No costly heating is required. Step-by-step directions also explain how to build a 7'0'' x 7'4½'' walk-in sunhouse, a window greenhouse, plus a hotbed frame. 114pp., 110 illus.

#612 HOW TO BUILD WALL-TO-WALL
CABINETS, STEREO INSTALLATION
SIMPLIFIED

As every stereo enthusiast soon discovers, a wall to wall bookcase and stereo installation can cost a bundle when done by others. This book not only simplfies building cabinets to fill space available, but also takes all the mystery out of installation of components. 130pp., 165 illus.

#613 HOW TO BUILD OR ENCLOSE A PORCH

Easy to follow directions simplify building a 12 x 16' porch or to size required. Enclosing an existing porch is also explained. Since codes permit this construction, it provides a fast and economical way of creating low cost living space. When enclosed with jalousies and screens, many porches double as extra sleeping areas. 82pp., 112 illus.

#615 HOW TO MODERNIZE A BASEMENT

Whether you create a family room or turn a basement into an income producing one bedroom apartment with an outside entrance, you will find all the information needed. It explains how to install an outside entry, build stairs, frame partitions, panel walls, lay floor tile and much more. 98pp., 135 illus.

#617 CONCRETE WORK SIMPLIFIED

This book explains everything you need to know to mix concrete, floating, finishing, grooving, edging and pointing, to setting ironwork and anchor bolts. It also explains how to waterproof a basement, install a sump pump, an outside entry and make all kinds of concrete repairs. 194pp., 257 illus.

#623 HOW TO REPAIR, REFINISH
AND REUPHOLSTER FURNITURE

Learn to apply first aid to ailing furniture. Reglue joints, replace webbing, bent and broken springs, caning and cane webbing. Everything you need to know from tacks to tools. Directions also explain how to build a studio bed with a nylon cord spring, decorate furniture with provincial trim, make picture frames, etc. 98pp., 138 illus.

141

#627 HOW TO MAKE CORNICE BOARDS, DRAPERIES, VALANCES, INSTALL TRAVERSE TRACK

Full size patterns simplify making cornice and valance boards, install traverse track, indirect lighting and much more. 66pp., 117 illus.

#630 HOW TO BUILD A SPORTSMAN'S REVOLVING STORAGE CABINET

Directions simplify building a glass enclosed gun cabinet, wall racks and a 24 x 72'' revolving cabinet that stores everything from guns to clothing. Learn to make what others want to buy. 98pp., 121 illus.

#630 HOW TO BUILD PATIOS & SUNDECKS

The Easi-Bild engineered patio roof insures a free flow of air, helps keep patio degrees cooler. Step-by-step directions simplify building to size specified or to size desired. Directions also explain how to build a sundeck, privacy partition, arbor and fencing. 98pp., 133 illus.

#632 HOW TO BUILD A VACATION OR RETIREMENT HOUSE

The perfect house for a vacation or retirement. One story with full basement provides two bedrooms and an amazing amount of useable living space. When built without a basement, it contains a bedroom, kitchen, bathroom and living room. An economical solution to today's housing costs. 194pp., 170 illus.

#634 HOW TO BUILD STORAGE UNITS

Easy to follow directions simplify building wall to wall storage closets with sliding, bi-folding or pivot hinged doors. Closets can be free standing, from floor to ceiling, or built-in. Directions also simplify building an under the bed storage chest on wheels, wall wardrobe and much more. 98pp., 145 illus.

#649 HOW TO BUILD A GARDEN TOOLHOUSE, CHILD'S PLAYHOUSE

Build a free standing or lean-to tool house and take all the congestion out of your garage. Over 100 step-by-step illustrations simplify building a 6'0'' x 8'0'' walk-in tool house, a 6'4'' x 4'3'' lean-to, also a 4'0'' x 5'6'' child's playhouse. Locked storage space accommodates bicycles, riding mower, all gardening tools, insecticides, fertilizers, seeds, etc. 82pp., 107 illus.

#658 HOW TO BUILD KITCHEN CABINETS, ROOM DIVIDERS, CABINET FURNITURE

Handsome pole type kitchen cabinets, room dividers, bookcases, stereo cabinets, desks and other needed furniture can be built by following directions offered in this book. Stock aluminum extrusions and prefinished plywood help amateurs make like pros. 98pp., 134 illus.

#663 HOW TO BUILD A TWO CAR GARAGE, LEAN-TO PORCH, CABANA

Building a garage can prove to be a richly rewarding experience. Letters from readers who built this garage confirm the task altered their outlook on life. Many who build turn it into an income producing singles apartment. 130pp., 142 illus.

#664 HOW TO CONSTRUCT BUILT-IN AND SECTIONAL BOOKCASES

Learn to build wall-to-wall bookcases. Frame a window, door or mirror. Build from floor to ceiling or to height desired. Every step clearly illustrated. Directions also explain how to build a room divider, free standing cabinet bar and other handsome pieces. 98pp., 137 illus.

#665 HOW TO MODERNIZE AN ATTIC

Everyone who wonders how they can meet ever rising living costs finds a timely answer in this book. It explains how to build stairs, insulate and transform an attic into a liveable apartment. Directions explain how to install a skylight, build partitions, install louvers, apply paneling, and much more. 82pp., 86 illus.

#668 BRICKLAYING SIMPLIFIED

All who seek income, peace of mind, an economical solution to a costly problem or employment in a trade where opportunity is unlimited, find this book a real guide to better living. It explains how to lay bricks, a wall, walk, veneer a house, build a barbecue, etc. It turns amateurs into pros. 146pp., 212 illus.

#669 HOW TO BUILD BIRDHOUSES AND BIRD FEEDERS

Encouraging a child to build feeders and birdhouses can stimulate a lifetime interest in woodworking. Full size patterns not only simplify building but also insure success. Helping a child turn a piece of wood into a useable and saleable article builds instant self confidence. 66pp., 86 illus.

#672 HOW TO BUILD WORKBENCHES AND SAWHORSE TOOLCHEST

To economically solve costly repairs and improvements, every home, apartment and place of business needs a workbench. This encourages those who build one to build others for resale. Simplified directions show how to build 6' workbenches, with a 6' vise on one or both sides, big drawers and tool compartments, to foldaway wall benches that require a minimum of floor space. 180pp., 250 illus., plus a full size foldout pattern.

#674 HOW TO INSTALL A FIREPLACE

Everyone who wants to install a woodburning stove, build a brick fireplace or install a prefabricated metal fireplace and chimney, will find all the direction they need. Installing a chimney completely within or recessed flush with an outside wall is clearly explained and illustrated. 242pp., 354 illus.

#675 PLUMBING REPAIRS SIMPLIFIED

Homeowners who dislike having their budget and peace of mind destroyed by a faulty plumbing fixture find this book helps save time, temper and money. Everyone who has learned to bake a cake or drive a car can easily replace parts and make repairs like a pro. Read, learn, then do what directions suggest and see how much more living you get out of life. 194pp., 820 illus.

#677 HOW TO BUILD A HOME WORKSHOP

In easy to follow, step-by-step procedure, this book explains how to build base and wall cabinets to fit available space. Having all tools stored where they can be used on a sturdy workbench encourages making repairs and building many needed projects. Directions also simplify building a trainboard storage wall, radiator enclosure and other useful projects. 98pp., 133 illus.

#679 HOW TO BUILD A STABLE AND RED BARN TOOL HOUSE

Measuring 20 x 30', this three box stall stable is easy to build while it makes a dream come true. Every step of construction, from having a reason to build (to create an individual and not a joiner), selecting a site, to building the cupola, is explained, illustrated and simplified. Directions also simplify buiding an 8 x 10' or larger red barn tool house. 178pp., 197 illus.

#680 HOW TO BUILD A ONE CAR GARAGE, CARPORT, CONVERT A GARAGE INTO A STABLE

Building a one car garage with ample space for a workshop, or turning a one car garage into a two box stall stable is clearly explained. Directions tell how to raise a garage to obtain needed headroom, build a carport, lean-to toolhouse and a cupola. 146pp., 181 illus.

144

#682 HOW TO ADD AN EXTRA BATHROOM

This complete, easy to read guide to home plumbing helps make a dream come true for only the cost of fixtures. In easy to follow directions, it tells how to make the installation and save a bundle. Those who don't want to do any plumbing discover sizeable savings can be effected by preparing the area, then having a plumber make the installation. Read, learn, save. 162pp., 200 illus.

#683 CARPETING SIMPLIFIED

Laying carpet in your home can provide the experience needed to do the same work for others. This book explains how a pro performs each step in words and pictures every reader can easily follow. Every type of carpeting, over every kind of floor, with or without padding, is explained, illustrated and simplified. Directions explain how to carpet stairs, install protective under the carpet electronic alarm mats, and much, much more. 178pp., 223 illus.

#684 HOW TO TRANSFORM A GARAGE INTO LIVING SPACE

Transforming a garage into a living-bedroom, with a kitchen and bathroom, can provide a safe and economical solution to a costly nursing home problem. It can also become an important income producer. Step-by-step directions assume the reader has never done any of this work and explains every step. 130pp., 139 illus.

#685 HOW TO REMODEL BUILDINGS

With abandoned big city housing units available to all who are willing to rehabilitate and occupy same, this book explains how tenants can become landlords with only an investment of time and effort. It tells how to turn an abandoned multi-family building, store, garage or warehouse into rentable housing. Every step explained and illustrated. Read and learn how to become a home-owner without spending a lot of money. 258pp., 345 illus.

#690 HOW TO BUILD BARS

Building a bar offers a fun way to furnish a recreation room. Learning to build a straight, L-shaped or any of the seven bars described provides an easy way to start a part or full time business. Doing something today you didn't know how to do yesterday broadens one's sphere of activity. 162pp., 195 illus.

#694 ELECTRICAL REPAIRS SIMPLIFIED

Learning to economically make electrical repairs not only generates peace of mind, but also income in your spare time. This book takes the fear, mystery and inflated cost out of many troublesome repairs. A special feature explains how to install wiring in a dollhouse. 134pp., 218 illus.

145

#695 HOW TO INSTALL
PROTECTIVE ALARM DEVICES

Recapture peace of mind by securely protecting all doors and windows with professional alarm devices. Learn how to discourage a break-in with magnetic contacts that automatically trigger a telephone dialer to the police, sound a loud alarm bell, instantly detect movement with easy to install radar. A layman's guide to professionally installed electronic protection. 130pp., 146 illus.

#696 ROOFING SIMPLIFIED

This "business of your own" book turns amateurs into professional roofers. Learn to repair or replace an asphalt, wood or slate roof; apply roll roofing, make a roofer's safety harness, walk and work on a roof with no fear of falling, plus much more. 130pp., 168 illus.

#697 FORMS, FOOTINGS, FOUNDATIONS,
FRAMING, STAIR BUILDING

This book tells every reader how to get into the building industry. Whether you build your own house, buy a prefab or want a career in building, this book tells everything you need to know about forms, footings, foundations, framing and stair building. 210pp., 310 illus.

#751 HOW TO BUILD PET HOUSING

Encourage all who love pets to build the shelter each needs. Learn how to build a doghouse, lean-to kennel, rabbit hutch, duck-inn, parakeet cage, an all weather cat entry, plus a unique catpartment that's easy to sell, easy to rent. 178pp., 252 illus.

#753 HOW TO BUILD DOLLHOUSES
& FURNITURE

To create a memory a little girl will never forget, build one of the three dollhouses offered in this book. Those searching for a part or full time money making hobby find a ready market for dollhouses. Full size patterns simplify making fourteen pieces of dollhouse furniture. 194pp., 316 illus.

#754 HOW TO BUILD OUTDOOR FURNITURE

Easy to follow step-by-step directions, plus a big foldout full size pattern, simplify tracing and cutting all parts to exact shape required. Learn how to build curved back lawn chairs, a matching settee, four passenger lawn glider, a chaise on wheels and much, much more. 130pp., 174 illus., plus full size pattern.

#756 SCROLL SAW PROJECTS

Helping everyone, a child or retiree, successfully turn a piece of wood into a handsome, useable and saleable article, builds the ego. This book insures success. 27 full size patterns permit tracing all parts, then assembling each in exact position shown on the pattern. 130pp., 146 illus.

#757 HOW TO BUILD A KAYAK

Simplified directions and full size frame patterns permit building this extremely light yet sturdy kayak to three different lengths, 14'3", 16'9" or 18'0". It can easily be carried on a cartop rack and used by one or two adults. Patterns insure cutting each frame to exact size required. 66pp., plus big, full size foldout pattern.

#761 HOW TO BUILD COLONIAL FURNITURE

Building colonial reproductions can provide hours of complete escape. You not only obtain furniture at a fraction of retail cost, but also enjoy every hour. Easy to follow directions and full size patterns simplify building a cobbler's bench, hutch cabinet, blanket chest, under the eaves rope bed, wall cabinet and other useful pieces. 12 colonial reproductions are offered. 258pp., 342 illus.

#763 HOW TO BUILD A TWO CAR GARAGE WITH APARTMENT ABOVE

All who seek an economical solution to a costly housing problem should read this book. It explains how to build a two car, two story garage. Directions also explain how to add a second story apartment to an existing garage. Space above provides a living, bedroom, kitchen and bathroom. Ideal for a single or couple. 194pp., 226 illus.

#771 TOYMAKING AND CHILDREN'S FURNITURE SIMPLIFIED

As every reader soon discovers, toymaking possesses a certain magic. Turning a piece of lumber into a whimsical rocking horse with a personality captures a child's imagination, triggers an interest in woodworking long before they have any idea how it was made. This book simplifies building 17 different toys and children's furniture. 194pp., 330 illus., plus a big foldout full size pattern.

#773 HOW TO CREATE ROOM AT THE TOP

If you need one or more extra bedrooms, or an income producing apartment with outside stairs, this book explains how to make like magic. Every step, from building a dormer, installing a skylight, building and installing inside and outside stairs to a second floor, is explained and illustrated. 162pp., 239 illus.

147

#781 HOW TO BUILD A PATIO, PORCH AND SUNDECK

Simplified directions take all the inflated cost out of building a front or back porch, a patio to length and width specified or to size desired, a carport and sundeck. Every step, from laying footings to installation of railings, is illustrated. Directions also explain how to make screens, porch repairs, swimming pool enclosure and much more. 146pp., 220 illus.

#792 HOW TO BUILD COLLECTORS' DISPLAY CASES

Learn to build handsome, clear acrylic, museum quality, floor, table top and wall display cabinets. These provide the perfect way to display every kind of possession from dolls, china, figurines, etc. Retailers buy these cases for store use as readily as for resale. 194pp., 229 illus.

#600 COMPLETE EASI-BILD CATALOG

Anybody can do anything if they follow directions offered in Easi-Bild Books and Full Size Patterns. The catalog illustrates hundreds of patterns and home repair and improvement books. Give this book to a youth seaching to find a career and many will soon be building everything from furniture, boats, garages to houses. Getting experience in their own home encourages doing the same work for others.

#804 HOW TO BUILD BOOKCASES AND STEREO CABINETS

Takes all the mystery and over 2/3 the cost out of building bookcases and cabinets to fill any available space. 194pp., 232 illus.

#811 HOW TO BUILD GREENHOUSES — WALK-IN, WINDOW, SUNHOUSE, GARDEN TOOL HOUSE

Of special interest to everyone who enjoys the fun and relaxation of growing plants the year round. The sunhouse appeals to sun lovers who enjoy sunbathing all winter. 210pp., 229 illus.

#758 HOW TO MODERNIZE A KITCHEN, BUILD BASE AND WALL CABINETS, POLE TYPE FURNITURE

Of special interest to every homeowner who appreciates the convenience and long term Capital Gains of a completely modernized kitchen. 210pp., 263 illus.

#850 HOW TO FIND A JOB, START A BUSINESS

Of special interest to teens, retirees and anyone who wants to earn extra income. Learn to offer what others want to buy. No capital investment required.

148

INDEX TO MONEY-SAVING REPAIRS, IMPROVEMENTS, PATTERNS AND BOOKS
(Number designates Easi-Bild Pattern or Book)

153

155

156

how to

FIND A JOB
START A BUSINESS*
Learn to Offer what Others want to Buy
No Capital Investment Required

Learning To Earn is a course few public schools presently offer. And even fewer have teachers experienced in the art of starting a business in today's highly competitive society. Regardless of past success, or successive failures, everyone who can read, and is willing to invest the necessary time and effort, can learn to lay carpeting, ceramic tile, build a fireplace or a house, if they follow Easi-Bild simplified directions. Since only the strong survive, developing interest in a skill or trade you enjoy, provides economic survival insurance.

This book is one of many that permits every reader to develop proficiency in a trade without leaving home. It explains how to lay carpeting like a pro, just as the other books explain paneling, kitchen modernization, buiding a one or two story addition or a one, two or three bedroom house. How you live depends entirely on what you are willing to do. Regardless of screwball national politics, only you are still in full control of your destiny.

If you want to economically solve a carpeting problem or go into business doing this work for others, read, learn, then get on site experience laying carpet in your home.

As this book goes to press, Easi-Bild's complete library contains 7842 pages and over 10,888 illustrations. Note complete list on pages 140 to 148, and the cross reference index to all patterns and books on pages 149 to 162.

Those who need low cost housing and all who want to make a sizeable long term Capital Gains without gambling, should

*Excerpts from Book 850

163

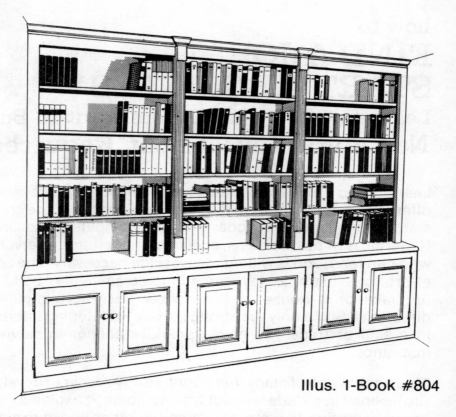

Illus. 1-Book #804

build a two car garage with an apartment above, or add a second story to an existing garage, as explained in Book #763. If your building site provides necessary space for this garage the distance local codes specify, don't let local zoning con you by saying, "We won't allow two family occupancy in an area zoned for single family housing." The Supreme Court ruled, in an East Cleveland, Ohio case, creating living space for a relative cannot be construed as two families.

This book makes one promise. It tells every reader, "What the author can do, so can all who follow direction." In no small sense, it transplants a second brain, an experienced guide that tells all who read how to do something they have never previously done. Without spending a bundle buying a "get rich quick franchise," it tells how to learn a new trade with only an investment of time and material.

164

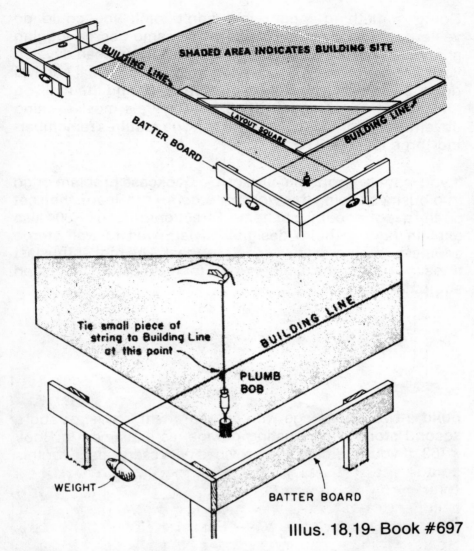

SHADED AREA INDICATES BUILDING SITE

BUILDING LINE

BATTER BOARD

LAYOUT SQUARE

BUILDING LINE

Tie small piece of string to Building Line at this point

BUILDING LINE

PLUMB BOB

WEIGHT

BATTER BOARD

Illus. 18,19- Book #697

Regardless of the past success or successive failures, everyone willing to invest the necessary time can learn to build bookcases and stereo cabinets like a pro when they follow the step-by-step directions offered in Book #804.

They can learn bricklaying when following directions offered in Book #668, Bricklaying Simplified; or get valuable experience in the building trades reading Book #697 Forms, Footings, Foundations, Framing, Stair Building.

Doing something today, you didn't think you could do yesterday, exercises the brain to the same degree jogging shapes up the leg muscles and lungs. Only you can develop your brain and body. Since economic and physical survival depends on how you use time, learning to find the real you and your true potential offers one of life's most exciting adventures. Getting to know the real you requires remembering three letters - TRY.

If you want to economically solve a bookcase problem or go into business doing this work for others, read, learn, then get on site experience in your home. Directions in Book #804 also explain how to build designer styled, wall to wall stereo cabinets. Each book has special appeal. The hi-fi enthusiast finds the handsome cabinets ideal for the most sophisticated equipment.

Illus. 1,2-Book #685

166

Your destiny is determined by how you use time. Sit on your butt watching TV and endless hours go down the drain. Invest the same amount of time doing something you have never done before and living takes on a new meaning.

Those who live in the city and lack transportation should read Book #685 How to Remodel. This is available from your public library, bookstore or direct from publisher. It tells how to turn an abandoned building into income producing apartments. As step-by-step directions explain, most cities give these abandoned buildings away for one dollar, or a small sum, and many agencies will lend funds needed to rehabilitate same.

Living space is in short supply and will get worse as the population expands and fewer new buildings are constructed. Learning to turn four walls and a roof into income producing living space offers unlimited opportunity. Regardless of age, sex, lack of experience or current financial status, others, just like yourself, have successfully done what the author says you can do. One reader wrote, "I just finished reading your book on "How to Rehabilitate Abandoned Buildings." I am pleased and impressed. I am a young woman who wants a home but just don't have the money since I am still paying school loans and high rent. I now have the courage to try doing it myself and your manuals will be my guide."

Another reader wrote, "I have Book #685, which (believe it or not) helped me to decide to purchase and renovate a 100 year old Victorian five story building that had been converted into a five-unit apartment building many years ago. While not available at $1.00 like a lot of brownstones in the area, it does need considerable repair to eliminate damage caused by termites, dry rot and fungus. Not having that kind of cash, I plan to "do it myself" and therefore need more of your books ASAP, especially #605, 606, 615, 617, 674, 675, 683, 694, 696, 697. I haved owned and operated rental properties for years, but never had to do more than paint and make small plumbing repairs. Now, thanks to your good books, I'll be able to do much, much more."

Just as a March wind or twister generates many customers for roofing repairs, so do the seasons of the year. Book #771, Toymaking and Children's Furniture Simplified, simplifies making easy to sell rocking horses, nine other toys and five pieces of children's furniture. Full size patterns in Book #771 permit tracing and cutting each part to exact shape required. These also provide painting guides that insure applying each color in exact position required.

An outdoor display of toys alongside a well traveled road, in a busy gas station, etc., invariably attracts sufficient customers to keep one person busy for a couple of months prior to Christmas.

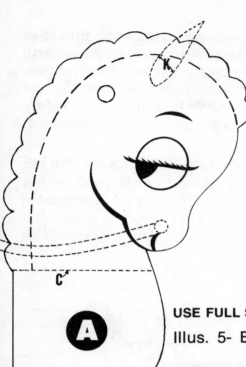

K

C

A

USE FULL SIZE PATTERN ON FOLDOUT

Illus. 5- Book #771

Illus. 3-Book #771

Those wanting to get into the roofing business should read Book #696 then phone each building material retailer and roofer. Inquire whether they need an able bodied roofer. Prior to making your first call, make a rope body harness and roofer's safety line and test it. Note how it insures safety when climbing a steep ladder, walking or working on a roof.

If no one has a job opening and you still want to get into the roofing business, do as every skilled roofer did in the beginning, advertise your services. Write or print up the same kind of message every roofer inserts in the yellow pages of a telephone directory. A quantity of 8½ x 11" circulars can be printed for very little.

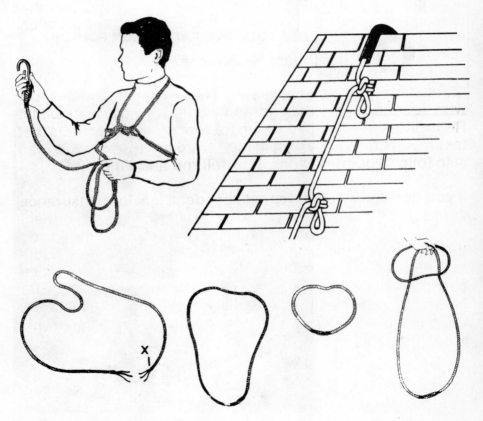

Illus. 3,4,5,6,7,8,-Book #696

170

Prior to or at the start of the rainy season, place one of these ads in every mailbox in that part of town where previous storms have done the most damage. Always place your message in the mailboxes where the property indicates the owner can afford to pay for services offered. Nature generates much fear and thus seeds many customers. Harness nature's power, she can be your best salesman.

If you don't own a home and have no place to test your skills as a roofer, still make the body harness and become thoroughly familiar with the roofer's safety line. When you phone an established roofer or retailer for an appointment, explain you are looking for work and you would like to talk to whoever does the hiring. The most favorable response invariably comes shortly after a storm has done considerable damage. Homeowners and pros give far more consideration when their need is urgent. In each interview with a homeowner, roofing company or retailer, speak up and say you know how to work and walk in safety on a roof and can make roofing and gutter repairs. This is a big plus especially with roofers. Few can find applicants with this capability. Regardless of what they say about roofing being a "trade that takes years to learn, your saying,"I happen to know but I can also follow your directions. You tell me and I'll do it."

If you decide to work as an independent, talk to an insurance agent. Find out what insurance you should carry to protect your customers against damage that may occur while you do the work. You must protect each customer. A knowledgeable homeowner will want to know the name of the insurance carrier, policy number and amount of coverage your insurance provides, before agreeing to your doing any work. In your ad, state you are a completely Insured Roofer. This helps generate confidence.

When visiting a retailer who sells roofing, note the product being offered. Read the step-by-step directions manufacturers supply. This not only gives you timely information concerning installation, but also more self assurance.

171

Learning to talk like a pro appeals to all who know their trade. Remember, what the author can do, so can each reader.

Another area that offers considerable potential is the tool rental store. Since they rent extension ladders, scaffolding and other special tools, they frequently have customers who need help.

Many have bulletin boards and outdoor display cases where they allow customers to advertise their services, even sell craftsmen products. If a tool store doesn't have this kind of display, but sees its potential, offer to build the bulletin boards and outdoor display cases.

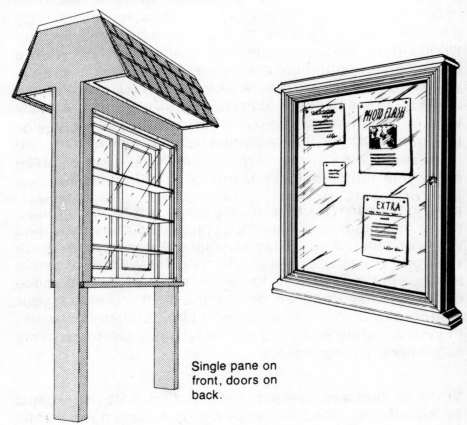

Single pane on front, doors on back.

Illus. 148,149 - Book #607

172

Those going into business should start as small as possible and should keep it that way until they feel completely dry behind the ears. Instant success can be as destructive to a small businessman as overnight fame can be to an actress. Everything that goes up can also go down. And those currently down have the same chance to go up. Today's unsound economy provides great opportunities for some, deep despair for others.

Like all Easi-Bild Books, this one offers every reader a chance to develop a whole new sphere of activity. As computerized research confirms, getting lucky just doesn't happen. It stems from experience, perseverance, and a will to try.

Consider these basic essentials: At birth we receive a body, a brain and an inheritance of time. How we use our body shapes our physical health. How we use our brain establishes a quality of life. How we invest time determines how well we will live. You may enjoy good health, possess an average or brilliant intelligence, but until you make the effort, and constantly do what needs to be done, you can't begin to enjoy your full potential. If someone in your family needs a job, or wants to start a part or full time business, READ, LEARN, THEN DO. With only an investment of time, capital to cover living expenses and needed material, this book opens doors to an experience called LIVING.

Any 16 year old high school student can easily follow step-by-step directions. Those who have no place to work, or money for material, can still gain valuable experience using scrap material most school teachers can easily obtain.

Since people are by instinct buyers of what they need, and constantly buy more of their daily needs than anyone really sells, showing a neighbor, doctor and others, what you can do, seeds many purchases of your services.

To be able to live a way of life many only dream of living, requires following a well established formula. Every Horatio Alger rags to riches story contains this formula. Each dreamed of what they wanted, then invested the time, thought and energy needed to materialize the dream. None were born with the needed experience. Each acquired this magical ingredient the hard way by following good direction and doing what needed to be done.

Investing one's life's savings buying a franchise operation is "strictly for the birds." It's frequently a faster way to lose than investing in the stock market. The safest investment anyone should make is time, money for material and tools plus living

Illus. 31-Book #756

expenses for as long as you can see any return on your effort. Each customer you sell is like a seed. Many have friends who will help spread the word about the service you offer.

Learning to turn spare time into an activity that can generate extra income has great therapeutic benefits. Everyone who makes Scroll Saw Projects offered in Book #756, discovers the activity can consume many sleepless hours.

If you feel tension building, start working with your hands, start making something you can sell or contribute to a church or charity fund raising auction. Remember, whatever price anyone pays for something you contributed is tax deductible, as your tax preparer will confirm.

If you live near a lake or navigable river, consider building and renting kayaks. This can prove a fun and profitable way to go into business. Book #757 explains how to build three different sizes, 14'6'', 16' and 18'. The book contains a full size foldout pattern that permits tracing each frame. These patterns insure accuracy and greatly simplifies construction.

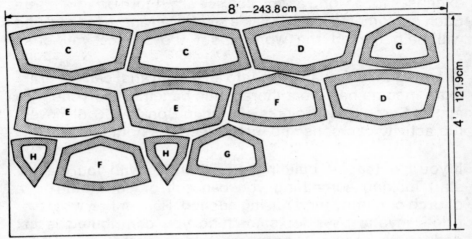

Frames for 16'9"

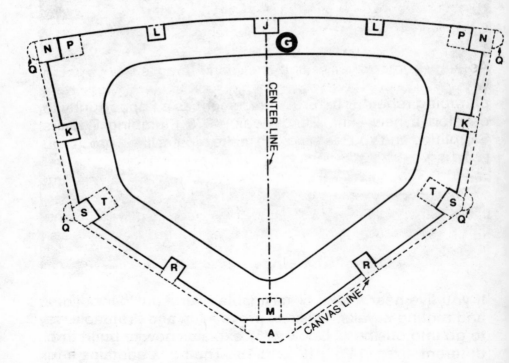

Illus. 11.28-Book #757

Always select an area you like, but make certain there is a local need for same. If you can't afford to build a house or a two car garage, but need one and would like to know how it's done, read the directions,then help a neighbor or friend build a comparable project. Or join an adult education class. Being able to get on site experience is important. Where this isn't possible, building a model helps clarify your thinking and does an amazing job of creating self confidence. Making any dream come true requires time, effort, hope in the future and prayer. All too many invest in hope and prayer, rather than in time and effort.

Those who can't afford to gamble on material needed to test their skill should contact adult education instructors or retailers regarding surplus scrap. You will be agreeably surprised to find many willing to help those who help themselves. Breaking into any new field of activity requires DIRECTION, then getting as much experience as possible. Offer to help someone for free to obtain this experience.

As every homeowner soon learns, something is always going wrong, always in need of a repair or replacement. Consider a plumbing repair or fixture replacement as an opportunity to develop a new skill. Read Book #675 Plumbing Repairs Simplified and you learn how to make repairs like a pro. If you need an extra bathroom, or only need to replace a fixture, read Book #682 How to Install an Extra Bathroom. Regardless of whether you need to replace a screw, washer, stem, faucet, sink, lavatory, tub or shower, Books #675 and 682 explain every step in words and pictures everyone can follow.

No matter where you live, your future is yours to shape. Transforming an abandoned building into liveable, income producing apartments, or providing a delivery service or protection for elderly residents in your area, as described in Book #695 How to Install Protective Alarm Devices, only requires determination and direction.

Learning to sell a service or product others want to buy, requires finding and filling a need at a cost the customer can afford and is willing to pay. The selling price must compensate you for both time and material. Going into business is something anyone can do. Being successful is another story. Survival depends on knowing how and selling to those willing to pay.

Earning sufficient income to pay living expenses, taxes, et al, takes ingenuity, imagination and initiative. Keeping your cool and learning to cope without blowing your top is something millions of successful people haven't mastered. Learning to live a normal span of years is one of life's most difficult lessons. Everywhere we look we see youth with a lifetime of promise being drained dry by drugs, alcohol or crime. We see associates drinking too much and enjoying it less. While learning to live may not be easy, why give up? The old adage, "Every dog has his day," is still quite accurate. While your day may not come for sometime, it could begin the very moment you began reading this book. As previously suggested, keep refocusing your mind's eye on direction you understand. Discover how time and good direction helps you achieve every goal you missed on a previous pass.

Relatively few people realize that time, labor, determination and direction can change the life they live, that everyone can be down one day and on the way up the next day.

MUCH GOOD LUCK!